ALI ROSS
ON SKIING

ALI ROSS
ON SKIING

WEIDENFELD AND NICOLSON   LONDON

To improve is to change. but to be perfect is to have changed many times.
John Pipe – one of my favourite pupils.

Published in Great Britain by
George Weidenfeld & Nicolson Limited
91 Clapham High Street
London SW4 7TA

ISBN 0 297 78970 8

Filmset by Deltatype Lecru, Ellesmere Port, Cheshire
Printed in Italy by L.E.G.O Vicenza

CONTENTS

ACKNOWLEDGMENTS

To my wife, Moira, for her enthusiasm and encouragement with this project and without whose skills at editing words, the writing of this book would have taken at least another five winters.

To Kjell Langset (Photography) for his skill and friendship, which made light of the difficult task of filming.

To my friend Ian McMillan for his skill as an artist and illustrator.

To Joe Bentley and everybody at Harrogate Ski Centre.

To Carrera (Optyl Eyewear Ltd) ski goggles and glasses suppliers, for ensuring that we could see when others could not.

To Nevica Ltd, whose ski wear made sure that we were warm, dry and visible.

To all at Salomon Ski Equipment (UK), who kept us extremely well-shod and safely-bound to our skis.

To Rossignol (GB) for supplying their range of skis for all conditions.

To my many old friends in Wengen, Switzerland, and in Tignes, France, who provided the facilities of their ski resorts with great generosity.

And to the many people over the years of my professional career who have helped form my teaching method.

7

PREFACE

I believe that virtually anyone has the natural ability to ski well. Yet many people who come to ski with me for the first time have frequently convinced themselves — or have been convinced by others — that they are 'only average skiers, who will never be *really* very good' (their words, not mine'). Their expectations about their own ability to improve have been gradually lowered over the seasons until they almost accept this limitation as fact of life. You may recognize the feeling: once you get beyond the first few weeks, you begin to feel stuck. This feeling can happen at any time, but sooner or later most skiers experience what seems to be an almost inevitable plateau. To me, this means above all that you feel limited; you perhaps feel that you can achieve more, but don't know how to. It is frustrating at best, and liable to make you give up at worst. Somehow the world of the expert seems as remote as the mountain peaks and just as difficult to reach. At moments like these, it is a world that appears destined to remain shrouded in mystery. We ski teachers, of course, make it look easy, so no wonder you get discouraged. But I believe that you'd be wrong to think that you will 'never be very good'. You can ski better than you ever thought possible entirely naturally, almost regardless of age, given a willingness to experiment with a few basic ideas.

This book is about those ideas and how I think you can use them to learn for yourself that you can overcome the limitations which hold you back. As the boundaries recede, you may find that your own ideas about what you want out of skiing will change. Skiers arrive in the mountains with all kinds of motives in mind — some specific others less clearly defined. Many people, indeed, start skiing without knowing exactly what attracts them to the sport. You may simply want to enjoy your holiday, skiing leisurely around the pistes or you may dream about venturing into the elusive places in the mountains far away from busy resorts. Whatever your reason, I believe that to get the most out of this magical sport, to discover the very special moments in skiing — in short, to explore how 'unlimited' you can be — you should understand first what *creates* good skiing. My aim is to help you to unravel the problems which stand in the way of that understanding. And then perhaps the places you've always dreamed of skiing will not seem so elusive after all.

1 LEARNING AND UNLEARNING

I started to learn to ski quite late – at the age of eighteen – but my fascination with the sport began years earlier on a stormy winter's night in the Highlands. Two Lovat scouts sought shelter in our barn and with them they had their skis – wooden, very long and elegant, and oiled until they shone. As an impressionable ten-year-old, I was spell-bound. Little did I know then that skiing would dominate my life in the future. In those days crofters' sons did not do such frivolous things. I did have a go at making my own skis the following day, by ripping two planks from a shed and nailing my father's wellingtons to them. Not having much of a clue about the finer points of ski design, I set off and promptly performed my first head-plant in the snow. That first painful encounter was swiftly followed by a second when my father discovered the hole in this shed and what had happened to his boots.

I didn't put on skis again until eight years later. The local golf course and the hills were my learning grounds. It was with the development of the Cairngorms that I got my first job in Frith Finlayson's ski school. By this time I was progressing through the BASI (British Association of Ski Instructors) system, learning how to be a ski teacher. I became a trainer twenty years ago, and over those years I have worked with everyone from absolute beginners through to trainee teachers and beyond to international racers. I am still learning. Yet still the same questions recur. How do all of these different people learn to ski? What are the things which stop them from learning? How do they manage to overcome these limitations?

Progress in skiing, I believe, comes not through the following step-by-step set pieces – 'now you can do snow-plough turns, lets move on to basic swings' – but rather through a thorough understanding and awareness of what is responsible for creating good skiing. If you look at how Alpine skiing developed, no one suddenly 'invented' a snow-plough turn and then a parallel turn. Parallel skiing evolved as the natural outcome of people just skiing faster once they'd gained some confidence. These developments were, however, soon labelled and analysed into parts and taught as sequential steps. 'First you do A, then B, followed by C. . . .' You may get the first, second and even third steps right, but then typically it all falls apart. Trying harder only compounds the problem. Despite this, it is still a commonly-used approach in many places. I believe that it is a particularly poor method when it is applied to skiing. Skiing is an activity which cannot be properly understood by simply trying to follow set-piece, technical instructions. Many people have experimented for years with other means of learning. In an effort to get away from convention, some have moved to other extremes and lost the balance of elements which contributes to our understanding what is happening when we ski.

Most of the problems, I feel, come from misunderstandings and misinterpretations of basic technical concepts at the very beginning, and these become interwoven with problems of awareness and perception. How do we overcome these problems? Many sports psychologists are fond of quoting observations like: we forget 90 per cent of what we hear, but we remember 50 per cent of what we see and hear, and 90 per cent of what we do. Amongst other things, this suggests what you may have felt for a long time, that ski teachers probably talk a lot to no great effect! However, simply 'seeing' may not be very useful as an aid to our own performance if we don't understand what *creates* what we see. For instance, if you watch a world-class slalom racer, you see a picture of flowing movements, which is often described as 'graceful' or 'effortless'; but this by itself doesn't help us to learn what creates the images we observe. Such visual aid can be actually detrimental if we misinterpret it. Similarly, 'doing' by itself is rarely helpful if we misunderstand what it is we're doing! So, before 'seeing' and 'doing' can become relevant to our learning, we must retrace our steps and return to basic technical concepts if we want to overcome the limitations imposed by these misunderstandings and misinterpretations. To do this, you may find that you are presented with a challenging prospect. To have come as far as you have along the learning path and then to be asked to go back and re-examine basics is not always easy. There is much 'unlearning' to be done.

In practice, this means that you should be ready to accept change, and that often makes people feel uncomfortable mentally. Physically too, change can present a challenge, especially when you've built up skiing habits over the years. Pupils sometimes say, when I've asked them to try doing something differently, that a particular position or manoeuvre feels strange and so it can't be 'right'. What you have always done in the past may stubbornly stay with you without you even being aware of it. Pupils are sometimes surprised to the point of disbelief if I tell them that their old habits are still there. Yet they can see when something is working or not for other members of the group. This, incidentally, is the reason I think video can be so helpful as a learning aid. Once people have got over the 'Oh, God, that's *me*!' reaction, they can begin to use it constructively. So to start with, developing effective skiing positions and movements will feel different from what you're used to, but with practice, it will soon feel normal.

Nothing changes from the most basic to the most advanced levels of skiing, I believe, if we learn effective techniques from the beginning. As you progress, you will need to modify your approach slightly, but the essentials remain the same. But you are no longer 'a beginner'. You may, as I said earlier, already have had several frustrating seasons behind you. You perhaps recognize the 'stuck intermediate' as yourself. Even if you think of yourself as an advanced skier, you may still wonder why you don't improve. So the notorious plateau is not confined to intermediates. It is some consolation, you may think, that racers feel it too.

'Intermediate' is a very broad label indeed; on the positive side, it is a certain measure of progress. On the other hand, intermediate skiers frequently find that they can get so far, and then no further. The problems most often manifest themselves after three to seven seasons. You may regard this as the inevitable result of only skiing perhaps two or three weeks a year. So intermediates may after several seasons be able to simulate what effective skiers appear to do, but never quite manage to ski as well as the people who taught them. I would define the 'intermediate' as someone whose misunderstandings or misinterpretations of basic techniques prevent him or her from progressing. But by rebuilding basic ideas, effective skiing will evolve naturally. Once you have understood what creates good skiing and have *felt* the ideas work for you, what you do thereafter will, with refinement, take you almost anywhere you want to go in the mountains.

I should like you to treat this book as a training programme, which you should intersperse with free skiing. But a word of caution here about what you understand by 'free skiing'. Sometimes, when I suggest to my pupils that they should go off and 'just ski' for a few runs, occasionally some of the group take this to mean that this is a chance to revert to the old habits which we're trying to get rid of! Free skiing to me means the opportunity for you to experiment with the concepts here, to

develop your own awareness of the point of the training exercises – *which are designed to give you the feeling of what I feel like when I ski.* They are not meant to be done as a penance and then forgotten about, as if they have nothing to do with skiing! I have no miracle cures and won't wave a magic wand. I think I sometimes surprise my pupils when I tell them that they shouldn't expect me to teach them anything! 'Instead,' I tell them, 'the onus is on you to learn.' I'm not playing with words. To me the difference is important. But I will try to help you to overcome the limitations which prevent you from improving. This book is one means of doing that. It is primarily designed to help the skier from intermediate level onwards, and therefore assumes that he or she has already acquired the elementary skills, although I hope that beginners who have already made their first tentative steps may find it an interesting book to read as well.

2 LIMITATIONS

There are things which can stand in the way of your progress before you even put on your skis; the effects of being in the mountains; being unprepared (this covers many possibilities, from not bringing the right clothes to not being physically fit); lack of awareness; our existing concepts about what is good skiing; fear of various kinds. The list is almost endless. You may experience some or all of these and could add to the list other things, no doubt. Let's look at a few of the factors and see how they can inhibit our skiing and what we can do about them.

THE SKIING ENVIRONMENT

People are often first attracted to skiing by its image in the holiday brochures, of blue skies and sunshine. But skiing is a mountain sport. This can and often does mean strong winds, snow and extreme cold. I have heard many skiers complaining when it snows, as if it is spoiling their holiday. I'm afraid I am not very sympathetic to this attitude. It is precisely this 'bad' weather which makes it possible to ski in the first place. You don't get very much skiing time if you wait only for the good days, so if you want to get the most out of your holiday, you should be prepared to encounter snow, poor visibility, cold and chill winds, as well as the beautiful sunlit days.

Having skied for more than a few seasons, you will almost certainly have experienced the alarming way in which the mountain weather can alter within a few hours or even minutes. I've spent years in ski resorts and learned to watch for signs of approaching bad weather, but unless you have special training, I don't expect most people to have the experience to do this. However, it pays to be aware of what you can be confronted with and to learn to *expect* the unexpected.

You will be better prepared for skiing if you learn about the inhibiting and, at worst, dangerous effects of cold and wind chill. Skiers frequently make the mistake of supposing that because the weather down in the village is still and warm, that the same will be true higher up on the ski slopes.

Temperature on average falls by about 1 degree C for every 150 metres rise in altitude. This means that, at a conservative estimate, you can generally expect the temperature up on the slopes to be at least 10 degrees colder than in the resort itself. There are other factors to consider too. Even if the air is calm, at 0 degrees C (quite warm for the Alpine winter) moving at quite slow to average speeds in skiing, up to 24 k.p.h., can have a considerable cooling effect on the body. Add to this lower air temperatures and a stiff breeze, and unless skiers are properly protected, there is increasing danger from frost-bite.

Wind chill chart

Wind or skiing speed (km/h)	Temperature (°C)																		
	10	7	4	2	−1	−4	−7	−9	−12	−15	−18	−21	−23	−26	−29	−32	−34	−37	−40
	Effective temperature (°C)																		
Wind still	10	7	4	2	−1	−4	−7	−9	−12	−15	−18	−21	−23	−26	−29	−32	−34	−37	−40
6 − 12	10	7	2	−1	−4	−7	−9	−12	−15	−18	−21	−23	−26	−29	−32	−34	−37	−40	−42
13 − 19	4	2	−1	−7	−9	−12	−15	−18	−23	−26	−29	−32	−37	−40	−42	−46	−51	−54	−57
20 − 28	2	−1	−4	−9	−12	−18	−21	−23	−29	−32	−34	−40	−42	−46	−51	−54	−57	−62	−65
29 − 36	−1	−4	−7	−12	−15	−18	−23	−26	−32	−34	−37	−42	−46	−51	−54	−59	−62	−65	−71
37 − 42	−1	−4	−9	−12	−18	−21	−26	−29	−34	−37	−42	−46	−51	−54	−59	−62	−68	−71	−76
43 − 52	−1	−7	−12	−15	−18	−23	−29	−32	−34	−40	−46	−48	−54	−57	−62	−65	−71	−73	−79
53 − 60	−4	−9	−12	−15	−21	−23	−29	−34	−37	−40	−46	−51	−54	−59	−62	−68	−73	−76	−82
61 − 67	−4	−12	−12	−18	−21	−26	−29	−34	−37	−42	−48	−51	−57	−59	−65	−71	−73	−79	−82

☐ No real danger to a properly clothed skier
☐ Danger − exposed skin would freeze in approximately one minute
☐ Great danger − exposed skin would freeze in approximately 30 seconds

What to wear is not, therefore, just a matter of fashion on the slopes – it is a vital barrier between you and the elements. You need clothes which will keep you warm and dry, if you want to ski in all conditions. To achieve this, it is important to have ski clothing which is waterproof and windproof. It used to be difficult finding clothes which were both *and* which felt comfortable to wear. Nowadays, skiers can wear a suit that uses a waterproof, windproof fabric, which *also* 'breathes', thus eliminating the stickiness which you felt with the old waterproofs. It is not an exaggeration to say that this fabric has revolutionized the comfort and safety level of mountain sports. The process works through a system of micro-pores, which allows water-vapour molecules to escape but which does not permit the passage of water molecules in. The end result is that you can ski in the worst weather and still remain dry. In the making of this book, I skied in all weather conditions, wearing suits (featured in the photographs) which use this type of fabric. I could stay out when others had to give up for the day.

FITNESS

Another factor which can seriously limit our skiing performance is our state of physical fitness.

Skiing is a particularly dynamic sport that is performed at high altitude, but down in the cities, modern life invites us to be sedentary. In other societies and times, our physical condition was important for basic survival. But nowadays, we have to make a special effort to incorporate fitness programmes into our daily lives. 'Getting fit' is a vague phrase. Not even the specialists agree on exactly what it means. But it does make sense to talk about fitness *for* something. The best-trained track athletes in the world, for instance, would not necessarily be fit in the right way for other sports.

Skiing makes special demands on our level of physical fitness. Try a fairly ordinary exercise such as running up a flight of stairs (or several, if you are already fit!). Then attempt running *down* the same stairs. What you noticed in all probability was that whilst you ran out of breath more easily going up, you felt a different kind of fatigue on the way back down – the stress was felt particularly in the leg muscles. Running downstairs illustrates the kind of *reactive* strength which you need when you ski. Few activities make similar demands in this respect. Add to this the unaccustomed effects of altitude and cold temperatures on performance and you can see why skiing requires special preparation. There is no doubt that you will get more out of your precious week's holiday if you train yourself properly, yet in this age of the health and fitness boom, I am still surprised by the number of people who set off for the mountains physically ill-prepared. Not only does this mean that they often spend the first couple of days nursing sore limbs, but also they stand greater risk of injury to muscles and joints.

What you're training is progressive conditioning to the demands of skiing. During exercise your rate of breathing goes up because you need more oxygen than you do when you're resting. But have you noticed how much harder you have to breathe when you are at altitude? This is the body's way of getting the oxygen it needs from the thinner air of the mountains. To help prepare your system as efficiently as possible for this, a general fitness programme should be the first priority. The benefits reach far beyond improving your physical condition alone. Recent university studies of different ways of training came to a thought-provoking conclusion. The most commonly-felt benefit was the least quantifiable, but the most tangible in the minds of the guinea-pigs. They all said that they simply felt better. Their general awareness of well-being was vastly improved. But to be of real value, your general fitness programme ideally should become part of your way of life. Whatever activity you choose, it should be something you can enjoy. There are many alternatives.

Running is one of the most natural forms of human exercise. It is also one of the least expensive. But if you are really unfit, then you can't begin with an athlete's training schedule. You must literally walk before you can run. Remember that you can start by leaving the car at home! There are many good specialized books which will advise you how to go about building up your running or jogging programme, so do consult them. You can incorporate exercises into your daily run to build awareness of skiing positions and movements. We often run 'slaloms' through the trees in Richmond Park or run slowly down hills, to build reactive strength.

You can practise angulation positions and movements by pulling against fences or leaning on trees! You can, of course, do these at home if it seems less likely to attract attention.

18

In any form of training, it is important to prevent boredom from setting in, so it is useful to vary your programme with alternatives. One which I use a lot – often as my main form of exercise – is cycling. It is easier than most to incorporate into the day's timetable, because you can use it as transport. Cycling will improve general fitness as well as increasing leg strength. It is often regarded as one of the best forms of exercise for skiing.

There is a special kind of cycling which should appeal to skiers in particular. It's called 'mountain biking'. For me, this had added much to my enjoyment of being in the mountains, covering forest roads, ridges and high passes in summer. But I use my mountain bike too just enjoying my normal cycling training in Richmond Park in late autumn. You can use them anywhere – going into the City, for instance. Cycling uphill is excellent fitness training for

skiing. This is where I think mountain bikes come into their own, because they will happily cope with tracks and rough roads that would be difficult for less sturdy bicycles. However far off the Tarmac roads you want to go, do stick to the already existing tracks. Remember to intersperse your training with faster sessions on the flat. Having said this, if the only means of training open to you is to cycle to work and back, then do it.

You may well have your own favourite sport or type of exercise that you can adapt in a way which is suitable for ski-fitness. However you do it, fitness training will reward you several times over for the initial effort.

Effective skiing also means that we need to extend our range of movements, making them more precise and swift, to enable us to react to the forces set up when we move downhill. To do this well, we require flexibility, agility and strength as well as overall fitness. These abilities are partly inborn, but can be improved enormously with practice. For instance, children have a huge advantage in flexibility, and although this tends to deteriorate as we get older, if we keep active we can maintain flexibility through exercises.

Do, however, consult a specialist for advice if you have had a recent or recurring injury, before starting on any new exercise programme. Start slowly to begin with, whatever type of exercise you choose, if you're unaccustomed to it. Gradual development of training is not only the safest way, but also produces the most long lasting results.

SKIING BEFORE YOU GO

Britain bristles with 'plastic' slopes. Artificial ski slopes have become immensely popular, and rightly so. Their aim, however, is not to ape snow skiing. What they *can* do is to provide a 'gymnasium' for skiers. Look at it this way: if you are a keen runner, for instance, some of your training may well involve circuits in a gym. It's not the same as running freely through the countryside, but then it isn't meant to be. The value of artificial slopes comes from being able to get the most out of your few precious weeks on snow by spending some time during your preparation practising skiing movements. I don't advocate just 'free skiing' in this respect, on a plastic slope – you don't have the freedom of the mountains before you, and just to ski on plastic without a proper training programme can be discouraging. Take advantage of the expertise of the coaching staff there and book some lessons. I believe that to use artificial slopes as part of the build-up to your skiing holiday will save you time and money in the end. A few sessions will save up to three days of your holiday on snow which would otherwise be spent just getting used to skiing again.

Harrogate Ski Centre.

FEAR

Fear can be the major reason that people feel limited in their skiing. By its nature, it is not always susceptible to logical solutions. What people often forget is that fear is sometimes a sensible warning device. We are sometimes right to be afraid. So never feel 'chicken' if you turn back at the top of a difficult run and descend by a less demanding path. There is no point in terrifying yourself and doing a lot of mental, if not physical harm, by attempting runs which are really beyond you, egged on by 'friends'.

However, fear is frequently so disabling that we cease to enjoy skiing at all. I have seen a lot of skiers who aren't that skilful technically, who get down by sheer bravado. They may well enjoy their skiing for a long time, but courage in the long run usually fails and then what do you do? I've also taught people who by their nature are quite timid, who once they prove to themselves how the skis and good natural technique will help them, are eventually prepared to take on the worst of the Alps' black runs.

I still experience fear when I am about to ski beyond my own limits – fear of the unknown. But I reassure myself that I know that the skis will do their work, given the right reactions from me. Knowing this over the years has enabled me to ski when fear alone might have been a deterrent. 'Knowing' in this sense succeeds in reducing fear to manageable proportions. There are other kinds of fear that can be put in perspective in this way. Fear of failure, fear of looking silly and fear of simply being seen to fall are a few familiar ones. Nothing succeeds in overcoming these limitations better than a good understanding of techniques. We *can* learn, then, not to be afraid: but

don't try to eliminate what I call the 'helpful' type of fear – natural caution has kept me alive in the mountains. Be aware that one day it may save you.

AWARENESS

An enormous problem for the two-week-a-year skier is that the movements used in skiing, though perfectly natural, often feel strange because you're not in the habit of using them. Living as many people do in urban environments, this is not surprising. You stand upright, you probably often sit in offices and so when you ski, you have to think again about developing awareness of what is being asked of you. We have to bend and modify the body's posture to cope with travelling at speed over rough terrain. We no longer feel 'normal'. We have to test our mental awareness in an unfamiliar and sometimes hostile environment. To have all of this said to you whilst you are no doubt sitting comfortably reading this book, is one thing. To be aware of how it translates into motion in the mountains is another.

STYLE

The dream of most skiers is to be able to ski anywhere, effectively. But often, we are in a hurry to be seen to improve. We want to look like good skiers first. 'Looking good' is often an aim in itself. 'What', one might well ask, '*is* style?' It is a question I often ask my pupils.

Too often, the impression of good skiing creates misinterpretations of the picture we see. For instance, an effective skier's performance

might produce the words 'elegant', 'graceful' and 'effortless'. All of these impressions are the effect of good techniques. By posing one's arms, legs and shoulders in a taught stance, one can arrive at a quite reasonable mime of good skiing, without skiing well at all. My question to you, the answer to which is developed in these pages, is a simple one. What is it that *creates* good skiing?

22

3 POSTURE

Problems of skiing posture are often self-correcting. By this I mean that once you have understood *and experienced* how the skis will work for you, a good basic stance tends to develop with no further instruction. However, there is something of 'a chicken and an egg' here, because whilst poor posture is often the result of misunderstood skiing technique, so also can one's technical progress be inhibited by misconceptions about stance or posture on skis.

What then *is* a good skiing posture? We walk around every day of our lives in a fairly normal, upright way. You've also probably had it drummed into you as a child to stand up straight and not to slouch. However, good posture for skiing is different. Our normal stance has to be modified quite a bit to produce a good skiing stance. This is because the demands of moving on skis over changing terrain, perhaps at a fair speed, mean that we have to flex and bend much more than we're used to. The body positions and movements which we need to adopt to produce effective skiing responses involve flexing the ankles, knees and torso. The legs turn into shock absorbers or springs, ready to adjust to different conditions.

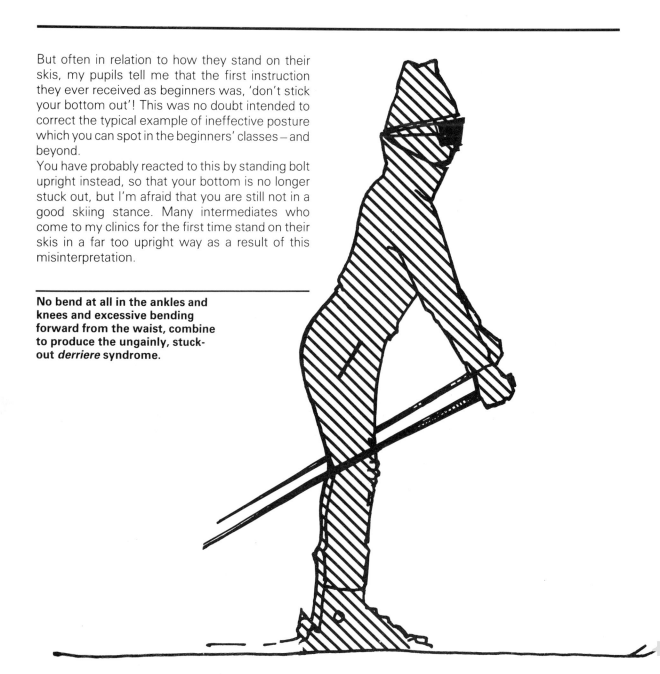

But often in relation to how they stand on their skis, my pupils tell me that the first instruction they ever received as beginners was, 'don't stick your bottom out'! This was no doubt intended to correct the typical example of ineffective posture which you can spot in the beginners' classes – and beyond.

You have probably reacted to this by standing bolt upright instead, so that your bottom is no longer stuck out, but I'm afraid that you are still not in a good skiing stance. Many intermediates who come to my clinics for the first time stand on their skis in a far too upright way as a result of this misinterpretation.

No bend at all in the ankles and knees and excessive bending forward from the waist, combine to produce the ungainly, stuck-out *derriere* syndrome.

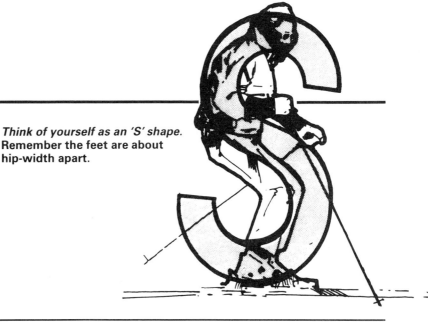

The problem cannot be corrected by simply 'not sticking the bottom out' and standing upright instead. What you should do is to rock forward at the ankles and knees.

Note the degree of bend at the ankles and the knees, with the shin pressing forward, feeling the front of the boot quite firmly. The body is still flexed at the waist to a certain degree. The overall image is of a good skiing stance.

Think of yourself as an 'S' shape. Remember the feet are about hip-width apart.

When I ask my pupils to experiment with this for the first time, nearly everyone is surprised by how much they need to bend and flex in the right places to give this good overall stance. It doesn't feel 'normal' to them. They say they feel almost 'hunched up'. However, this doesn't mean that it's wrong.

Here is an exercise that I have used for many years to increase awareness of posture. You can experiment with it almost anywhere. Try it standing on the flat first, stationary, then find a gentle slope, think about it before you set off and then just try straight running downhill. Experiment by stretching up as high as you can and then crouching down low. Get the feel of the range of movement possible. If you grade your most upright position as 10 and your lowest as 1, then a reasonable position for skiing would be between 5 and 7. It will vary depending on your own physical conformation.

WATCHPOINTS

When you bend at the waist, beware! It should not produce a hollow lower back. Hollowness here inhibits the movements you need to be able to make to ski well. *Remember* – think of the 'S' shape.

To me, having spent years on skis, this stance has become second nature. If you visualize the image of good posture every time before you set off downhill, until you do it automatically, you may be surprised how much your general skiing will improve. Good posture in skiing, though, is only the beginning. When we're moving, our positions and movements in skiing, I believe, are entirely natural reactions to the dynamics of skiing, and not actions which can be taught. Given the right conditions of feedback, the body will adopt quite natural positions without being given specific set instructions about what to do.

4 CONCEPTS

The problems which many skiers face, and which stand in the way of progress, have much to do with our concepts of what is happening when we ski. And that often means how we understand the concept of turning. To be able to turn effectively in skiing is vital if we are to control the rate at which we go down the mountain, and to decide where we're going. When we see a good skier making elegant turns in full flight, the picture is one of effortlessness. But to simply try to copy that picture without knowing what creates it, means that we are often reduced to mechanical misinterpretations.

To understand any kind of turn, from the snowplough to the parallel, we should first look at the most important factor in skiing – the ski itself.

THE *SKI* WILL TURN *YOU*

Very often, the attitude of skiers towards their skis is not a very charitable one. Skis are seen as hostile planks to be forced around the turn, too often seeming to go where *they* want to, and not where you would rather go. They take on almost human characteristics if you listen to half of the complaints about them.

Yet fundamental to any understanding of modern skiing is one point, which once explained, understood and most importantly, felt to work by pupils, utterly transforms their feelings about their skis and indeed skiing itself. The point could

hardly sound more simple and it is by no means a new discovery, but I never cease to be amazed that most people spend their entire skiing lives never having heard it. From the time that Alpine skis were first used, the ski has been designed as a turning machine. *It* will turn *you* – if you know how to use it.

Over the years, skis have become very sophisticated turning machines indeed, with huge amounts of skill, time and money invested in developing them further. The essential characteristics of the ski, though, have not changed.

Hold your skis up and look along their length.

What you see is a graceful curve – the ski's 'side-cut'. Wide at the heel and tip, narrower in the approximate middle. This curve will vary according to the type of ski, but its function is essentially the same in all skis.

Side-cut is the key to the modern ski's turning abilities. Other important factors also influence this, but for the time being let's concentrate on how you can make the ski's turning characteristic work for you.

Very simply, on the move, when this ski is put on its edge and pressure is applied, it will bend in an arc and carry you round with it, as if you are on rails.

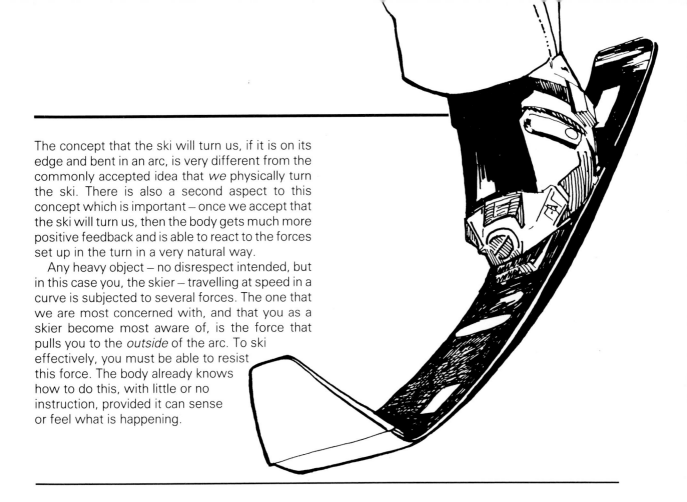

The concept that the ski will turn us, if it is on its edge and bent in an arc, is very different from the commonly accepted idea that *we* physically turn the ski. There is also a second aspect to this concept which is important – once we accept that the ski will turn us, then the body gets much more positive feedback and is able to react to the forces set up in the turn in a very natural way.

Any heavy object – no disrespect intended, but in this case you, the skier – travelling at speed in a curve is subjected to several forces. The one that we are most concerned with, and that you as a skier become most aware of, is the force that pulls you to the *outside* of the arc. To ski effectively, you must be able to resist this force. The body already knows how to do this, with little or no instruction, provided it can sense or feel what is happening.

FEELING THE FORCES

Look at some other sports, for a moment, in which people make movements that are identical to those of a good skier, without being taught how to. There are two sports in particular like this, which are carried on far away from mountains – roller-skating and skateboarding.

You only have to watch the dynamic youngsters performing slaloms on the concrete of the inner cities at high speed, to be reminded immediately of top competitors in skiing. The secret for the roller-skaters is that they get positive feedback from their own turning machines through friction between the wheels of the skate and the pavement and this gives the body the information it needs to react to the forces involved with an entirely natural movement. No one ever teaches them how to do this. What is also interesting is that if it rains, producing a slippery surface, many of them say that they don't even try to skate – they get a negative kind of feedback that tells them that they no longer feel secure. After all, who wants to fall on concrete?

Look at these pictures. Notice the movements and compare them to those of a good skier. You don't need to take up roller-skating or skateboarding to be able to prove for yourself that you can adopt a position as good as that of the skier in the picture. Just try this simple experiment at home. It is one which I will be using quite often.

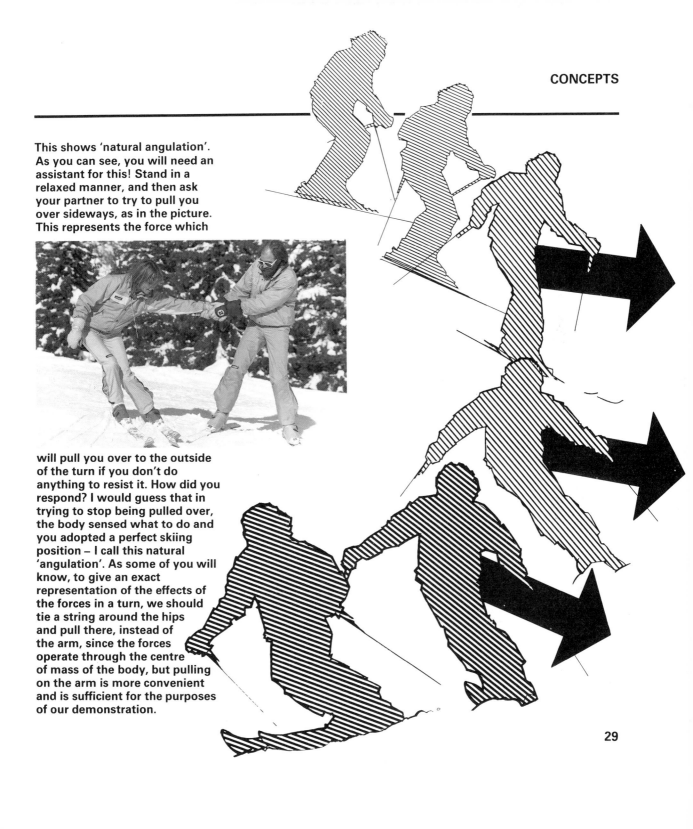

This shows 'natural angulation'. As you can see, you will need an assistant for this! Stand in a relaxed manner, and then ask your partner to try to pull you over sideways, as in the picture. This represents the force which will pull you over to the outside of the turn if you don't do anything to resist it. How did you respond? I would guess that in trying to stop being pulled over, the body sensed what to do and you adopted a perfect skiing position – I call this natural 'angulation'. As some of you will know, to give an exact representation of the effects of the forces in a turn, we should tie a string around the hips and pull there, instead of the arm, since the forces operate through the centre of mass of the body, but pulling on the arm is more convenient and is sufficient for the purposes of our demonstration.

29

So if the body knows how to ski, why do we need to be taught?

I believe that the answer is quite simple. In the very nature of skiing, we are standing on a sliding base on a relatively slippery surface. (Remember the skaters who wouldn't train on a wet day?) Since there is much less friction, the body receives confusing information. It doesn't like the feeling of what I call 'stereo motion' – moving forwards and sideways simultaneously, especially at speed downhill.

You recognize that insecure, unbalanced kind of feeling if you happen to step unexpectedly on a patch of ice in the street. In skiing, if our concept of turning is to push the skis around the turn, skidding the heels, then we only tend to increase this existing feeling of insecurity. Indeed, I feel that this way of turning contains the very ingredients which land us on the 'plateau'. It limits us to being able to ski only in the ideal conditions of a perfect piste, blue skies and sunshine. Should either aspect of these ideal conditions not prevail, the performance of most recreational skiers will probably deteriorate quite drastically. Take away the blue skies and sunshine and replace them with howling blizzards and poor visibility, or remove the perfect piste and in its place put ice, deep snow or bumps and many skiers have problems. Let me explain why. In perfect conditions, even if we turn by forcing the skis into a physically-induced skid, the skis will work for us by default. They sink slightly into the packed snow, and don't skid too much so the body gets some positive feedback, enabling us to cope – we feel happier and less unstable.

On ice, however, this idea of turning produces excessive skidding, which makes us feel afraid and generally out of control. In deep snow, there is resistance to the skis skidding sideways, and so trying to turn by this means doesn't work. You are reduced to leaping the skis around if you can, and in any event, getting very tired and falling a lot.

On the other hand, if our concept of turning is to use the skis to turn us, travelling in curves along the edges – the feeling is like being carried around on rails – this creates much more positive feedback in *all* conditions, good and bad. The body then can respond by angulating naturally and thereby resisting the force generated in the turn. This necessary edging of the ski, often called 'carving the turn', is almost always regarded by experts as a technique for advanced skiers only – even just for racers, according to some opinions. I believe that holiday skiers are not only *able* to use this concept of turning at their own speeds and level of skill, but also that *unless* this basic 'edging' principle is learned, they will be limited in their skiing progress. The degree of 'carving' or 'skidding' in a turn should depend on one thing – the level of skill of the skier and not a totally different concept of turning.

5 EXPERIMENTS

To understand the basic concepts which I have been describing is only the first small step. For you, the skier, what is essential is to experiment with the foregoing ideas and to develop physical awareness of how they unfold in practice. The problem is that you already know how to ski a different way: you have already built up skiing habits which by now may be highly ingrained. So in this first experiment, I am going to ask you to 'short-circuit' the brain and see what follows.

Try the exercise in a stationary position first of all. Stand in a narrow plough and put one hand firmly behind each knee, at the side, and then really *press* the knee progressively inwards, first to one side and then the other. Try to get the feel of rolling the knees over to each side. Notice how the legs and the hip lie inwards.

Now find a gentle slope, preferably one that you know and that has a run out at the bottom, so that you can concentrate on the experiment. Again stand in the shallow wedge with your hands on your knees as before and let the skis slide down the fall line, allowing yourself some speed. Then press one knee inwards, progressively. If everything went well when you pressed the knee inwards, you felt that you were being carried around in a curve – the ski working for you.

Try it again pushing the other knee. Don't worry at this stage if one side feels better than the other – we're all one-sided to some extent.

It isn't necessary to hurry at this or at any other stage. Just practise this for as long as necessary to give you the feeling of the skis working.

Now link up the turns, so that when you've felt the ski carry you around in one direction, relax, let the skis run a little and then try the other direction.

Remember that I suggested a *shallow* plough or wedge. Not a feet-together parallel and not a beginners' braking snow plough. The reason is that when you're trying to manoeuvre like this at relatively low speeds, you need the support of the inside ski to stabilize you and to give you the confidence to try something new.

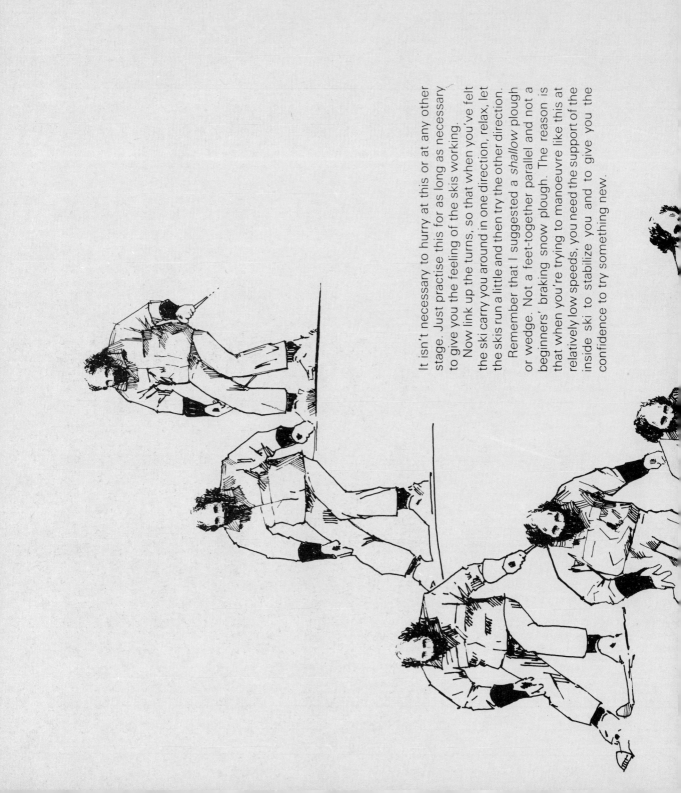

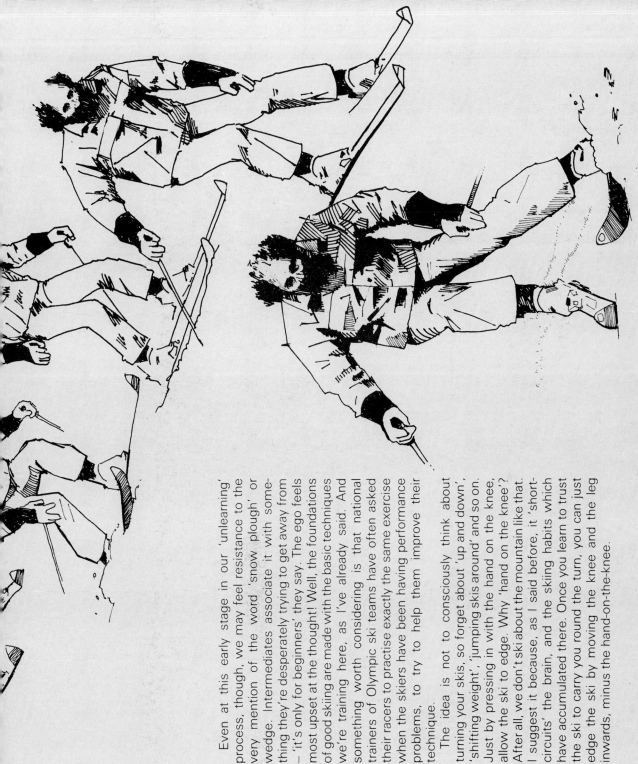

Even at this early stage in our 'unlearning' process, though, we may feel resistance to the very mention of the word 'snow plough' or wedge. Intermediates associate it with something they're desperately trying to get away from – 'it's only for beginners' they say. The ego feels most upset at the thought! Well, the foundations of good skiing are made with the basic techniques we're training here, as I've already said. And something worth considering is that national trainers of Olympic ski teams have often asked their racers to practise exactly the same exercise when the skiers have been having performance problems, to try to help them improve their technique.

The idea is not to consciously think about turning your skis, so forget about 'up and down', 'shifting weight', 'jumping skis around' and so on. Just by pressing in with the hand on the knee, allow the ski to edge. Why 'hand on the knee'? After all, we don't ski about the mountain like that. I suggest it because, as I said before, it 'short-circuits' the brain, and the skiing habits which have accumulated there. Once you learn to trust the ski to carry you round the turn, you can just edge the ski by moving the knee and the leg inwards, minus the hand-on-the-knee.

Problems

I would be surprised if at this stage some of the old habits hadn't crept up on you, even in this basic exercise.

Resist the urge to turn!

The problems in trying this for the first time are often caused because we react defensively to something new. Take the word 'turning' itself. It has strong rotational implications. You interpret this to mean that *you* do the turning. Now, I am asking you to rethink this. But until you feel it working for you, you're not entirely convinced that it will. Or at least part of you is not. You may well intellectually understand that an edged and pressured ski will turn you, but another part of the brain is used to relying upon what is ingrained and so despite yourself, you may try too hard to turn, especially through the fall line, and then find some of the following problems cropping up.

Body rotation

This means the whole upper body turning in the intended direction of travel – before you have given the skis a chance to turn you. This is the gremlin which isn't going to be convinced that the ski will do it instead. The effects of this can be interesting – inner-ski catching, ski tips crossing and generally skis getting into a tangle.

Weight shift

You've been conditioned into doing this for years, so it comes automatically. If you're standing normally (no skis!) and someone tells you to shift weight, then you do what comes naturally and transfer your weight on to one foot. Trying to do this on skis, on the move, simply results in moving most of your weight over to one side and flattening the turning ski, with unpleasant results. Since the ski is now skidding excessively, you feel insecure.

A too-wide plough or wedge

Starting off with a wedge which is too wide – like a beginners' braking plough – means that as we edge the turning ski, the other is still on its inside edge and it catches. Going too slowly can produce the same effect.

In a narrow wedge, the lying inwards of the leg and hip to create edging will automatically allow the inner ski to follow the turning ski.

Ski skidding at the end of the turn

The turn began well, but finished with the ski skidding away from you at the end – not a nice feeling. What has happened is that you have forgotten to follow the movement through, by pushing the knee in progressively – this means increasing edge – throughout the radius of the turn. Remember that the force pulling you to the outside will get stronger towards the end of the turn and if you don't resist this, the turning ski will break away – the force got you!

Try counting your way through the turn if it helps you to remember that the emphasis is on progressively edging the ski. The turn is an arc. Segment it like half of the face of a clock. The beginning of the turn is at twelve o'clock, and its end is at six o'clock. The fall line is at three o'clock, by which time the ski will already be well on its edge.

FASTER AND FASTER

Once you feel completely happy with the aim of the hands-on-the-knees exercise, you will automatically – maybe even without noticing it – be travelling faster. By this time you are confident enough to be edging the skis without the assistance of the hands on knees to remind you. Remember, though, that speed means that the force is more liable to get you unless you're ready for it. Simply, the forces generated in the turn, as I explained before, are greater at higher speeds, so you have to remember to make more committed edge-changes at the beginning of the turn and to remember that greater *reaction* is necessary towards the end of the turn.

WOBBLY KNEES

As you gain confidence, you can try a variation on the previous 'hands-on-the-knees' experiment. It is fun and is excellent preparation for the faster reactions needed in more advanced skiing. I call it the wobbly-knees exercise.

Start again in a shallow wedge, with the hands on the knees, on a friendly slope, but one long enough to allow you to develop a bit of speed. This time we're going to push the knee inwards several times during the radius of the same turn. A positive push then release, push then release until you have turned enough in one direction, then relax into a neutral position and repeat the process to the other side.

Try not to be too ambitious with the number of knee pushes you try on each side, until you get the feel of it! It's quite a committing manoeuvre, since until you become used to it, the effect of releasing the edge after each push can feel a bit unbalancing.

The mobility which this exercise trains is essential, for instance, in fall-line turns and coping with moguls.

There are many variations on this experiment which you can invent for your own amusement.

6 FROM CATERPILLAR TO BUTTERFLY

THE PARALLEL TURN

I don't think I will forget some of the worst parallel turns I have ever made. They happened during an 'Interski' conference, a meeting of the ski-teaching nations of the world. During these meetings every country is put through its paces, from elementary steps to advanced skiing. The demands of the parallel-turn demonstrations, with the top ski-nations watching, added to my fear of letting the British team down and produced what I felt to be the most posed, stiff performance that I've ever made.

'Parallelitis' is an affliction that affects most skiers at some point. The symptom is that you want to pull the skis together in an attempt to create the appearance of stylish skiing. Often, as well, parallel skiing is used as a measure of your ability by others – in ski school, for instance – and you too probably regard it as a yardstick. It is the dream of every intermediate to perform perfect parallel turns all over the mountain. There is so much emphasis on it that it's no surprise that you try to copy what you see – the appearance of legs and feet coming closer together. But mistaking the effect – the skis and legs coming closer – for the cause will only produce what I called earlier the mime of effective skiing.

Parallel skiing, to me, is entirely a *result*, produced by speed and effective technical performance. You cannot learn to ski parallel simply by physically bringing the skis closer together.

Amongst the illusions that inhibit the intermediate skier's progress most, this interpretation of what parallel skiing involves comes close to the top of the list. So what is responsible for creating a good parallel turn?

The explanation is to be found in the effect of forces again. As you speed up, the force pulling you to the outside of the turn is greater. This creates more pressure on the turning ski and less on the inside ski, which will drift inwards towards the turning ski.

So the effect – the legs coming closer together – is purely a *result* of what is happening as we ski faster. The usual misinterpretation arises because we think this effect is produced by the physical *action* on our part of bringing the skis together. Just remember as you go faster, greater *reaction* from you is needed to resist the force pulling you over.

Remember the 'pulling-over' exercise. Try it again. You have to react with greater movement – inwards with the legs and hips to the centre of the turn, away from the pull – as the force increases. If you do the same on the move, in skiing, you will find that as you go faster you will be skiing parallel naturally without thinking about the relation of one ski to the other.

The parallel turn (right).

There is only one difference between the snow-plough turn and the parallel turn – *speed*. You may have noticed when you've been practising the exercises given earlier in the book that as you skied faster, the wee wedge you began with gradually narrowed and the skis started to come closer together. It was no accident: you were skiing parallel naturally without consciously bringing your skis together and without anyone telling you 'now you must ski parallel'. Nor was this a game or a trick to get you to ski parallel without thinking about it.

For many years, I've used a variation on the 'pulling-over' exercise to give pupils a feeling for the greater reactions needed when they ski faster. But try to bear in mind the point of these exercises, especially as your skiing improves. I have said before, and will stress again, that these activities, which we call 'exercises' are designed to give you the awareness in different ways of what it feels like for me when I ski. They are not meant to be done and then forgotten about as if they were unrelated to the 'real' business of skiing.

This variation is really the pulling-over exercise on the move. I call it 'reaching-out'.

Reaching Out

What we did first time was to simulate the force in the turn by getting someone to pull you over if they could. You resisted by adopting a perfect skiing position. If you recall that image and compare it to the skier in the photograph above, you may see a remarkably similar position.

Visualize the positions and movements you made then. Instead of standing still on the flat and having someone pull you over, we're going to introduce the real thing – moving downhill.

Find a fairly wide, gentle slope. I say this because it is testing enough to try to unlearn old

39

habits and to experiment with new ideas without being inhibited by the terrain. Move off from a fairly shallow traverse to start with, in a narrow wedge again, and as you feel yourself picking up some speed, reach out as far as you can with your arm to the outside of the turn, stretching as if to touch the slope and draw an arc in the snow. (If you're trying this on an artificial slope, you'll just have to imagine drawing on the bristles.)

Remember that the reaching out must be progressively greater throughout the turn. When I ski I do feel that I'm reaching out as much as this, so if it feels odd for the first few attempts, don't mistake this feeling of strangeness for doing something 'wrong'. Unlearning will often mean that simply because you're trying something different, you will no longer feel 'normal'. It doesn't mean, though, that it isn't right.

The feeling this exercise produces has often been described by pupils as being – 'very secure and stable'. 'In control' is another description.

With practice, as you go faster, the small wedge you started with will disappear after the first couple of turns. At this stage you can experiment with different things – changing the radius of the turns, making a few longer ones at the beginning, then tightening them with quicker, sharper reactions. Count through the long turns slowly, if it helps, then count quickly through the shorter turns.

Experiment with sounds. During the filming of 'How We Learned To Ski', I was wired up every day by the sound recordist and when I heard the play-back in the evening, I was surprised to realize that I often made my own accompaniment to the movements of skiing. 'V-R-O-O-M-M' meant the long turns; 'VROOMM' equalled short turns. Yet I hadn't been aware that I was doing this at all.

Problems

Habits die hard. Often what you've done before may persist without you being aware of it. So none of the problems that can occur at this stage should be seen as disasters without solution. Some of the problems you may experience, indeed, have much to do with old habits creeping up on you.

The symptoms may be varied – skis breaking away at the end of the turn, hips turning outwards, shoulders swinging around uphill, to name just a few. To me, these have remarkably similar causes.

Taking the first symptom, if the turning ski breaks away from you towards the end of a turn – it is skidding, in other words – the feeling is that somehow you have to stop it. What you've often been told is to put 'more weight on the downhill ski'. But all this does, if you actively try to put it into practice, is to flatten the turning ski, it loses its edge as a result and skids even more.

Secondly, if you find your hips and shoulders swinging around uphill, the corrective answer you've heard many times is to 'look down the valley'. But to simply twist your upper body and shoulders around in that direction will not correct the cause of the problem.

The crucial key to overcoming all of these habits can be found in this one exercise.

Imagine that there is at the centre of the turn a wee seat – about hip height – which you're going to try to sit on.

Really try to project yourself on to it. When you get this right, with the ski on its edge, the hips – the centre of mass – will automatically be placed to the centre of the turn all the way through. As a result, the problems described above will begin to be resolved. But you should try it and feel this for yourself.

41

At this stage in learning, there is no substitute for your commitment to experiment with these ideas. But you must take care not to be put off by a static understanding of what happens when you are moving and already, therefore, under psychological pressure. At the start of the turn, for instance, I feel that I have to commit myself by projecting my knees and hips towards the fall line – otherwise how would I turn? But unless you're used, as I am, to trusting that the skis will take you through that 'panic zone' as you reach the fall line, then I realize that you will not find it easy until you prove it for yourself.

Here is an exercise that besides testing your degree of commitment, will help your parallel turns enormously. It is quite an advanced form and you can't do it slowly.

Start first in a steep traverse across a wide run so that you gather speed. Then begin to run along the top (upper) edge of the upper ski, by adjusting more pressure there. You should still keep the other ski on the snow. Now for the commitment. Whilst you hold the pressure on the upper edge of the top ski, project the upper knee downhill. If all goes well, the feeling you get is of an instant response, almost unexpected. The ski whips you around very quickly.

If it doesn't work to start with, you can be sure that this tells its own tale. In most people, especially under stress in skiing, there is a strong desire to turn regardless. We get all the expected results of this: flat skis jumped around, rotation of the feet, everything *except* a simple edge change – which is all this exercise is trying to show.

THE POLE PLANT IN THE PARALLEL TURN

Poles are usually the computer punch-cards which say 'now you've *got* to turn', so you stab the snow, hang on and hope that a turn will happen as a result. I call this the lamppost effect. A candid videotape of the use of poles by most skiers would produce quite an interesting visual aid about the huge variety of misinterpretations possible. Even to the untrained eye, its obvious when someone has got it right (see pp 43–7) and even more obvious when they haven't.

1

2

4

5

6

7

The pole plant can cause problems if we haven't anticipated enough the impact of the pole hitting the snow. The body will be rotated if we don't stiffern the arm to take account of this. Just remember that at the time you plant the pole, this action should not affect the body's position.

Much is written about precisely where and how to 'plant the pole'. And to you probably a lot of it isn't very helpful. Amongst the many variations on offer about the 'correct' way to do it, there is agreement on one thing at least. The pole used properly is of enormous help in parallel skiing and beyond. Equally, it is of no help whatsoever if used incorrectly. Worse still, it can be a positive hindrance.

If you've tried skiing *without* poles, you can begin to see why they're useful. You feel odd without them, you feel less balanced and as people have often graphically said, you feel like a cat without whiskers. So they *can* be useful just as antennae and balancing aids.

But we want to know how they can positively help in the turn. Commitment, as you know, is especially important at the beginning of the turn. The *most* committing movement is when we change edge to start our next turn. As you are by now aware, until you get used to it the feeling is that you almost launched yourself into space – actually towards the fall line. This is where the pole can be helpful. At the crucial point of changing edge, the pole will give you support. This timing is more important than exact directions about where you put the pole.

When people first come to ski with me, I never mention use of the poles. In fact, I often tell pupils *not* to use them. Usually, as confidence grows, pupils ask about these seemingly redundant appendages, if they haven't already begun to use them themselves quite automatically, as an aid to turning.

I sometimes ask my pupils to find a very gentle slope, where they can run out easily and just practise straight running downhill, planting the poles rhythmically. The same thing can be tried on a traverse, first to one side, then the other.

Remember that you're moving forward and you will notice that the moment you plant the pole, there is a jolt in your arm from the impact of the pole plant on the snow. This will rotate you unless you resist it by stiffening the arm and 'ride over' the effect.

Don't worry too much about where the pole should go. There are so many factors that affect this, that there is no definitive rule for everyone. Length of pole, body build, speed, type of terrain all play their part.

A problem at this stage can be rotation from not stiffening the arm when the pole hits the snow. Lack of anticipation of this effect is often responsible. Holding the pole too loosely can often result in a feeble action. Don't be afraid to hold the pole *firmly*, especially at the crucial time of impact.

Remember too that since the direction of our next movement is towards the fall line, the pole plant shouldn't get in the way of this. Planting the pole too closely to the ski, blocks the movement we need to make at this critical stage. It will help if you think about remaining *open* to the fall line.

Misconceptions

Parallel skiing is subject to many misconceptions that are frequently directly responsible for much confusion and failure to make progress. These misconceptions often arise from how conventional instructions are interpreted by the learner. In this section I would like to examine some of these problems, in the light of what I have said in the last chapter.

'Ups and downs'

You have probably come across the statement that skiers make 'up and down' movements. You probably think of this as you might do in normal, every-day life – if someone tells you to 'go up and then go down', I'd guess that you might stand up straight and then bend as if you were going to sit. You've followed the instruction perfectly. And if that was how I thought 'up and down' movements happened in skiing, then I wouldn't be able to ski either!

It is true that when we watch a good skier, we see increases and decreases of height – the 'ups and downs', presumably. But what creates this effect? Not the straightening and bending described above, but something else. The result – the ups and downs – is produced by the body's natural responses to the forces generated in the turn (see pages 50–2).

We angulate during the turn, reducing height.

1

At the beginning of the next turn, we return to a neutral position, thereby increasing height. This gives the impression of the skier making 'up and down' movements.

2

Remember that the effect – ups and downs – is produced by the body's natural responses to the forces generated in the turn.

5

52

'Shifting weight'

Another common misconception is that: 'You must shift your weight to the turning ski.' This is probably the most used and misunderstood instruction of all. It is easy to see why. You walk down the street every day in life, shifting your weight from one foot to the other without thinking about it. And so, is it surprising that when it comes to skiing, you do what comes automatically? As an illustration, I ask my pupils to 'shift their weight' and everyone follows my instruction to the letter. They stand on one foot. In skiing too, they interpret this command to transfer weight as they would if they were walking along the road, shifting their weight from one foot to the other.

It is true that when you ski, pressure distribution changes. In America, they have even tried to demonstrate this by putting pressure-sensitive pads under the skis and wiring them up to show that there are increases and decreases of pressure throughout the turn. But what I would like you to think about is who – or what – is responsible for this pressure distribution? And secondly, how useful is it as a skier to be told to actively 'shift your weight'?

To describe this point again we're using the 'pulling over' exercise. Stand feeling reasonably relaxed in a good skiing stance, with your weight balanced over both feet. Ask someone to take hold of your hand and pull you over sideways, gradually increasing the pull. Remember that this produces a similar effect to what progressively happens when you are subjected to forces in the turn.

Before you begin, try to be aware of where the pressure is and then notice how it changes as the pull increases. If you visualize this in skiing, you will probably say that pressure is gradually increasing on your turning ski.

Now I have a question to put to you. 'Who was responsible for this "weight shift"?' Try the experiment again if you aren't sure. How many of you, I wonder, said that *you* were responsible for it? H'm. If you did, then try the same experiment again, but this time deliberately transfer your weight over the 'turning ski' (the foot nearest your helper!) and ask to be pulled over again. As the force increases this time, you probably found it almost impossible to stop yourself falling over. You couldn't resist the force.

What this proves, if you think about it, is that the problem arises because you have 'shifted your weight on to the turning ski', as you were told to do, but all this does is to flatten the ski and make it next to impossible to resist the outward pull in the turn. What the demonstration tries to show you is that the 'weight shift' is a *reaction* and not a deliberate *action*. Weight distribution is, in fact, *resultant* – the result of resisting the forces in the turn effectively.

'Unweighting'

This brings us to yet another widely misunderstood phenomenon in skiing – 'unweighting'. It is conventionally accepted and taught that a parallel turn is initiated by unweighting the skis. So much emphasis is placed upon this phase of the turn that it is even described as the 'magic ingredient' of all advanced manoeuvres. My view is that if, up to now, we have required the ski to be on its edge, with pressure applied to it before we can turn effectively, then it does not appear to make a

53

great deal of sense to argue that weight should be actively taken *off* the ski in order to initiate a turn. As we have already seen, parallel skiing evolves naturally, as a result of greater speed and movement, using exactly the same concept that we introduced at the very beginning. What is important is *edge change* in initiating turns.

Here is a little food for thought. If you are travelling in a traverse at 10–15 m.p.h. and you 'unweight' your skis, what happens? When I put this question to my pupils, the response is frequently less than certain. If you simply 'unweight' your skis, you will carry on in the same direction — traversing! Inertia has the effect of keeping you going in the same direction all things being equal. *You will only change direction when you change edge.* Another question I should like you to consider is, if we understand how the ski works for us when it is placed on its edge and pressure is applied to it, how can it do this effectively with the pressure removed from it? We know that pressure distribution changes, so it may be said 'unweighting' happens, but as we have seen so often in other discussions, this phenomenon is a *reaction* and not, as popularly understood, a deliberate *action* on the part of the skier.

Effective skiers *do* feel greater pressure on the turning ski, especially as the forces increase at higher speeds, in a World Cup slalom, for instance. But if we follow the instruction to 'shift your weight', then all that happens is ineffective action.

When we are static, our weight acts straight downwards. When we are moving, especially in a turn, this alters. Instruction is often given to us when we are stationary, but in a dynamic state trying to put instruction into effect, the results are often not what we expect.

'Parallel skiers ski with their feet and legs together'

That good skiers ski 'with their feet and legs together' is a notion that is less widely accepted nowadays than it was in the past. Modern skiing has moved on to the idea that to ski with your legs and feet glued together is not actually a very effective way of getting down the mountain. But it is still a prevalent misconception amongst many skiers. It is often seen as a 'stylish' way to ski. As I explained earlier, this one impression alone has been responsible for more anguish and failure to improve than almost any other.

Physically closing the feet together simply produces a simulation of effective skiing.

It is true that good performers appear to ski with their legs close together, but remember what is it that creates this appearance – the effects of speed and of angulation.

Note the angulation of a good skier – leg lean, i.e. legs and hips to the centre of the turn. The legs appear to be close together.

If you look at the photograph here you will see what I mean by this.

By catching hold of the skier's arm and trying to pull her over, I represent the force which will pull you to the outside of the turn, if you don't do anything to resist it. In trying to stop me from pulling her over, the skier has adopted a naturally angulated position, with the feet about hip-width apart. Yet also note how the legs appear to be together.

Remember that in skiing, this is a natural reaction to speed and the forces set up in a turn. It is not created by the physical action of bringing the skis together. The appearance is caused by the legs and hips having moved towards the centre of the turn to resist the outward pull.

Now try this. It is the same experiment, but this time whilst exerting the pull, I ask the skier to physically *close* the feet together. It is now impossible for her to resist the force and I find it quite easy, without any increase in force whatsoever, to pull her over. I have tried this exercise with all kinds of pupils, including some very strong ones, and the effect was always the same. I advise you to try it for yourself at home in order to get the feel of it.

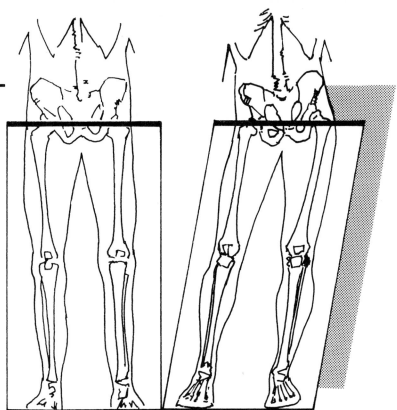

The body, then, can resist the outward pull with the feet at hip-width apart, but finds it very difficult to do so indeed when the feet are close together. Why should this be so? Look at the diagrams on the right.

In the first diagram (1a) we can see that a human being's relaxed natural stance is determined by the width of the pelvis. It is my contention that by leaving the feet at hip-width apart in skiing, we can achieve more effective leg lean, because what I call the 'parallelogram' (see diagram 1b) is maintained — the hips remain at more or less the same height, permitting easy and natural angulation.

In the second set of diagrams, showing the feet close together, our 'parallelogram' becomes an elongated 'triangle'. When we try to lean the legs inwards with the feet in this position, one hip

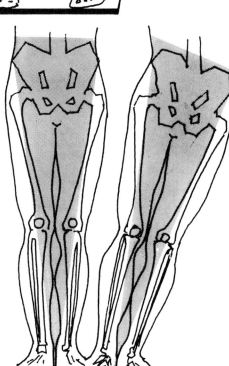

drops lower than the other, making angulation much more difficult.

So, what does this mean in skiing terms? When you can resist the force, as in the first case, this means on skis an effective body position, with the ski being held well on it's edge, curving throughout the turn. It produces a feeling a great stability, a bit like being carried around on rails.

In the second experiment, with the feet held deliberately close together, this represents an ineffective skiing position, with the skis skidding excessively, and resulting in a very insecure feeling for the skier. It is clear that physically bringing the skis close together limits that skier's performance.

Remember what we said in the chapter 'From caterpillar to butterfly'? The skis *will* come close together quite naturally as you go faster.

An added problem for you, the pupil, is often that the people who give the impression of feet and legs clamped together can often be the professionals themselves, who ski every day in winter and perhaps for a large proportion of summer too. They can also be locals who have skied that particular mountain before they could walk. I was once asked by a sceptical journalist, 'Can they all be wrong?' No, they're not wrong, but the observer's superficial interpretation often is. I explain this by what I call the 'skill threshold'.

This threshold can be decided by many things – fitness, mental state, terrain and experience on skis. Most holiday skiers, for instance, are lucky to have two or three weeks' skiing a season. Without being unkind, such a person's threshold is liable to be fairly low. Outside of that good day, blue skies, sunshine and a perfect piste, perhaps you begin to recognize that skier? You feel you need all the help you can get.

It would be surprising if your ski teachers couldn't make skiing look easy. They could ski with their feet and legs together almost anywhere in their native terrain, in any weather. I can ski with my feet and legs clamped together too, when I have to. But when I do, I feel that I am performing at about 40 per cent below potential. And I believe that most skiers are not very different, whatever their level.

Throw most of us down a top downhill course and the feet and legs together 'style' soon disappears. The threshold for racers, for instance, is much higher than average: their limit may be reached at 60 m.p.h. instead of 30 m.p.h., but it is still nevertheless a limit. After this limit has been reached, they too will begin to look and feel less polished. How many racers do you see in the extremes of competition skiing with their legs and feet stuck together? Yet *within* their thresholds, they can do so very easily on runs that most of us could only ski slowly if we were to ski like this.

Very simply, to force your skiing into this pose – or any stylized pose – I believe, is to limit your potential.

'Good skiing looks effortless'

This is not so much a misconception, but rather an impression which is easy to misinterpret. I agree that good skiing *does* look effortless. There can be few more beautiful sights in sport than a good skier in full flight through deep powder snow, a bump field or simply making flowing turns down a wide open run. The truly skilful performance has tremendous aesthetic appeal, so it is understandable why you should want to copy it. But how *do* you copy 'gracefulness', 'elegance', 'effortlessness'? These words describe a picture, but as I have suggested already, such visual aids are of

little use to us if we just try to imitate what we see, without knowing first what *creates* what we see.

The impression of 'effortlessness' is actually quite an accurate description of good skiing, because technically efficient skiers use a minimum of physical input. Less skilful skiers use physical strength to force their skis to turn. The good skiers know that the ski is designed as a turning machine; when it is placed on its edge and pressure applied, it describes an arc, which carries the skier around. What creates the image of effortlessness is the positive feedback from the edged ski that allows the skier to feel the forces set up and then react to them with perfectly natural movements.

7 FALL-LINE SKIING

3

If parallel skiing has been a frustrating goal for many skiers, then linking parallel turns straight down the fall line has been another source of probably greater frustration. As we have found so often before, how you misinterpret what you see is responsible for many of these problems. Looking at the sequences of pictures on pages 62–3 and 64–5, apparently the feet are being pushed from side to side. But if you try to copy this, you will at best only succeed in producing a simulation of fall-line skiing. And again, you find that you become limited to where and when you can do this. Every variation of fall-line skiing produces essentially the same illusion.

If you were on a chair-lift above a good skier making fall-line turns, you could see that the skis were following their length around the fall line and not, as it may appear, that they are being physically pushed by the skier from side to side. The turning skis *carry* the feet to either side.

Before I go any further, I would like you to consider something for a moment. As you move on to more advanced skiing, you aren't being asked to perform something which is completely different from what went before. Many skiers believe that snow-plough turns are an inferior species, different in kind from parallel turns, and that more advanced parallel turns are at yet another remove from both. But from the most basic to the most advanced forms of skiing, nothing changes I believe. How we apply our technique is modified slightly, to take account of speed, terrain and faster reactions, but the essentials remain the same.

Let's take a look at the parallel turns we've been practising so far and at the tighter variation which we call 'fall-line' turns.

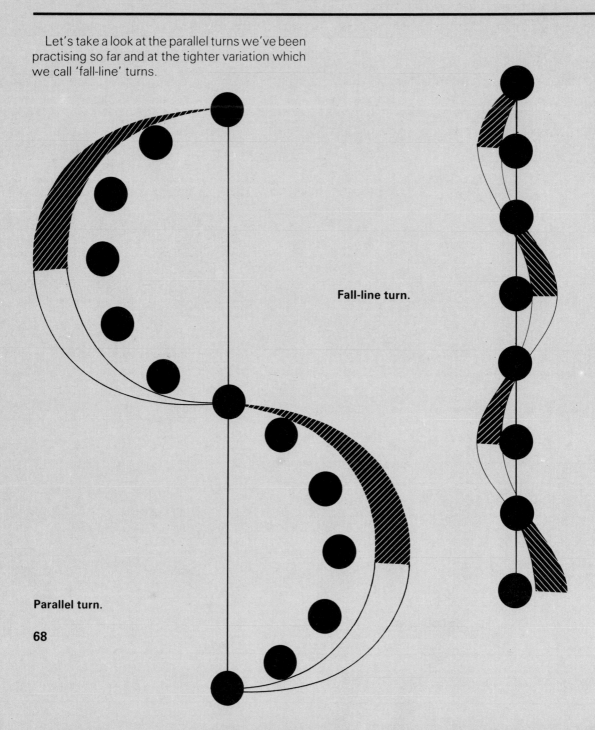

Fall-line turn.

Parallel turn.

Long parallel turns mean turn, traverse, turn, traverse.

Fall-line turns eliminate the traverse. We commit ourselves to the next turn at the moment we finish the last one. The difference is this. In our long parallel turns, the body is following in the same direction as the skis. In fall-line turns, the body is moving in one direction – straight down the fall line – **whereas our skis are turning either side of that line, crossing the body's trajectory.**

What happens is that providing you stabilize the upper body, the turning effect of the skis causes energy to be progressively built up in the legs. 'Stabilizing' means keeping the hips and shoulders facing down the fall line and so resisting the turning effect which the skis have on the body.

Our natural balancing aids – the arms – also help us in this. As the turn finishes, your body's direction of travel crosses that of the skis, the built-up energy is released and helps you to change edge by projecting the legs from the end of the last turn towards the fall line. A firm pole plant can be a very effective aid to this release of energy. It also helps to stabilize the upper body. To describe the dynamics in fall-line skiing, I use what I call the 'rubber block' effect.

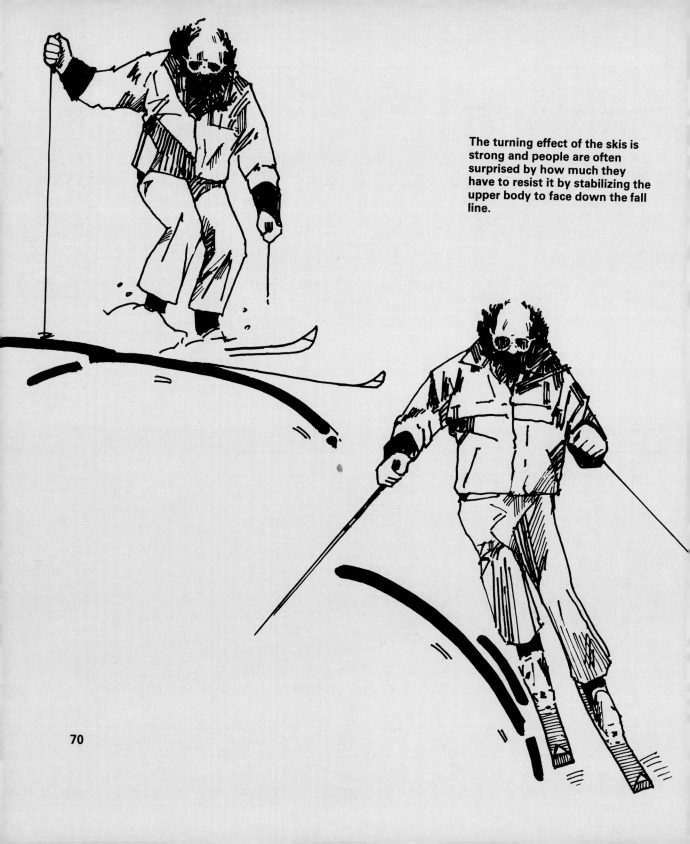

The turning effect of the skis is strong and people are often surprised by how much they have to resist it by stabilizing the upper body to face down the fall line.

Fall-line skiing takes practice, but we have nothing that is really new to learn. Although movements need to be quick and precise to react to the stronger forces involved, they are not different from what you've already done. The initial inward movement of the knees and hips puts the ski on its edge and the follow-through progressively keeps it there. In fall-line skiing, ideally the energy build-up is released so that the edges change without any effort on your part. But as before, to become aware of the degree of movement needed, we return to basics. The wee wedge will help you to get the feel of moving straight down the fall line, without traversing.

Choose a moderate slope, one on which you feel comfortable. This time, try the hands-on-the-knees exercise which we used before, making the knee movements sharper and stronger to lighten the radius of the turn. Remember to coordinate the inward movement of knees with that of the hips. If the terrain which you've chosen is not too difficult, you should be able to make tighter turns than you've been used to. I must stress that to get effective control in the fall line, we have to use stronger and sharper knee movements. The 'knee-wobble' exercise is excellent for training the right reactions here.

Problems

Until you get used to the feeling and effects of skiing in the fall line, there a few common difficulties which most skiers encounter to start with.

I sometimes find that it helps to remind ourselves of why we want to master fall-line skiing. There are times and places when long turns won't do. On steeper slopes or narrow tracks and gullies, for instance, fall-line turns are often all we can perform if we're to get down at all. So they're an essential part of skiing, which enable us to go virtually anywhere and tackle most of the more difficult terrain which you're likely to meet in the mountains.

A frequent problem when people try fall-line turns for the first few times is that they allow the hips and shoulders to be turned in the direction of travel of the skis. The torsional or 'block of rubber' of energy is lost and the next turn has to be started by physical force. Imagine holding a fairly large eraser rubber as if you're going to wring it. Twist the bottom half as far as it will go, then release it. It springs back. It is this kind of creation and release of energy which helps us to make effective fall-line turns. Visualize the force pulling you down the slope, from the centre of your body, and follow this line of force.

You should be able to feel the skis 'shooting' forward as the energy is released, so that the edge change takes place almost automatically. This effect replaces strong physical input.

Since rhythm is important in fall-line skiing, the pole plant causes problems when it is badly-timed. But don't get too obsessed with it. We can detract from our overall performance much more by insisting on the correct use of the pole. Feel happy with your turns first and the pole will often naturally come into use almost without you thinking about it.

Above all, don't expect too much too soon. Remember that this is a training programme and can't be hurried. Training takes place in any sport gradually, so don't rush into practising fall-line turns first thing in the morning. Have a couple of warm-up runs first, covering the progression of

exercises on undemanding terrain. Sort out what it is you want to work on, think it out, visualize yourself doing it, and lead into it easily. Only then are you ready. And at the other end of the scale, if it's just one of those days when nothing is working and you feel that you've been practising for hours to no great apparent effect, then know that it's time to stop for the day.

72

8 SHORT SWINGS

As you become more adventurous you may seek out greater challenges – or you may just find yourself one day on top of an unexpectedly steep part of the mountain. Perhaps there is no other way to descend; or the path may be too narrow even for side slipping, that great 'last resort' technique, when the alternative is blind panic. At moments like these you may realize the usefulness of being able to make very tight fall-line turns – 'short swings' in professional jargon. These are probably open to more misinterpretation than most aspects of skiing.

Again, we have nothing that is really new to learn. What creates our impressions is essentially always the same. How we apply our understanding needs to be modified to suit the demands of speed and the terrain, but remember nothing really changes.

You have probably seen people performing short swings on flattish slopes and thought that they were doing an exercise in jumping the skis from side to side. Some of them may have been! But this kind of misinterpretation often leads people to practise jumping up at the beginning of the turn, which is *not* what creates what you see.

In good, tight, short-radius turns, the impressions we have of the skis being jumped around are created not by the skier actively leaping to start the turn, but rather by effective reactions to the demands of turning down a steep slope. On steep slopes, there will be a degree of skid and edges need to be set sharply if we are to control our descent effectively. It is the *rebound effect*

from the set edges which creates the impression of the skier 'jumping' (see pages 74–7).

It's true that there is more physical effort required in short-swing turns. But this input is channelled purely into making sharper, stronger movements to tighten the radius of the turn and to check the end of the turn by setting the edges. Done effectively, the rebound effect is quite strong, and almost bounces the skier towards the fall line and into the next turn. All the effort, in other words, goes into the *end* of the turn, not the beginning. The rebound or the apparent 'leap' is pure *reaction* to the more powerful forces involved. The pole is a great prop on steep slopes, so use it. It is an invaluable aid to lean on as the rebound takes place. Do remember that you need to hold the pole quite firmly – really grip it – otherwise it will never produce the effect you want.

To practise awareness of the movements needed, go back to the wee wedge for the first few runs, on a moderate slope again, where you can develop some speed, but not so much that you feel inhibited. Ski down the fall line, pressing the knee inwards strongly, pause, letting the skis run up to a count of two and do the same to the other side. Resist the urge to physically turn your skis to control your speed. After the first few turns you will realize that the most secure way of achieving this is to make more progressive movements more quickly. Now experiment with shortening the pause. Reduce it to a count of one, until it becomes obvious that you don't need to do

1

2

3

4

5

6

anything except make a definite edge change, immediately after the end of the last turn.

Use the terrain you have to play with the idea. If you are lucky enough to be in a resort that gives you access to a long, long reddish run, without bumps – what I call cruising skiing – then you have an ideal laboratory.

Begin with long turns, tightening them into fall-line turns, then really try to sharpen the knee movements. If you have a short, quite steep slope, with a flat run-out, then practise setting the ski edges and *really* using the pole. If you're prepared to experiment, there are many ways of developing the feel for tighter turns.

At this stage, it is worth remembering that even though you've advanced a long way, things will still go wrong. Tight fall-line turns have a nasty habit of highlighting the shortcomings in even the best performers. New misunderstandings are unlikely to be the cause. What is more usual is that old problems concealed at the earlier stages drop their disguises.

Problems

As short swings demand quite energetic responses, the main problems revolve around how we react to more powerful forces on a steep slope.

Over-rotation is one common problem – the hips and shoulders swing around with the skis. It manifests itself in different ways, but one of the commonest is that the lower ski breaks away.

Often, in edging the skis, we remember the necessary knee movement, but forget that the hip has to go with it – leg lean is impossible otherwise. Do you remember the 'wee seat'? If you only move the knee in and don't coordinate it with the hip movement, then the result is, more often than not, that the hip rotates outwards and ski edging is lost.

Over-rotation is also due to not anticipating the stronger forces at the end of the turn – recall the early explanations. We are dealing with higher speeds, steeper terrain and stronger forces, but the fundamentals haven't changed.

Timing and rhythm of movements can often go astray when you first try short turns on steep slopes. These are important, but again are the result of effective technique. You can only learn it by practising and by not being too concerned about getting it absolutely right.

Psychologically, it is often asking a lot of your commitment to trust what is happening when you're confronted with a steep slope, so the tendency is to force the skis around regardless, rotating physically and causing all sorts of unpleasant results.

9 BUMPS

Few recreational skiers can look down a field of large bumps or moguls happily and many feel more than a little anxiety if there is no other way down. Bumps are high on the list of the most disliked conditions, yet they can actually help us turn if we know how to use them (see pages 78–81). To begin to understand how we can learn to cope with bumps and even enjoy them, we need to know how they were formed in the first place (continued on page 83).

1

4

Very simply, moguls are formed by us, the skiers. The passage of many pairs of turning skis carve tracks into the snow which get deeper and deeper until a perfectly manicured run, flattened by the piste machine overnight, is transformed within a morning to an intimidating mass of looming hillocks. How big they eventually become is decided by the number of skiers, how skilful they are, the steepness of the slope and the depth and condition of the snow. It's no accident that all other things being equal, the biggest moguls appear on the steepest runs. Although that is not a thought which is likely to be very comforting if you find yourself at the top of such a slope.

The 'skiability' of bumps is also affected by these same factors, so that if you arrive at midday after a new fall of snow on a bump slope, most reasonably effective skiers can manage quite easily. But one day later, after the ski-school classes and less skilful skiers have struggled down, the picture of the bumps looks very different. What was a good 'line' the previous day has been completely altered because the round smooth bumps have become nasty, square and icy. This tends to happen because many skiers often find the existing line too committing, so they side-slip a few bumps. This squares them off, and scrapes away the snow from the downhill side so that the fronts of the bumps become icy. This is why several top American resorts have a check-point at the top of perhaps two or three selected bump fields to ensure that the standard of skiers is high enough not to destroy the line of the bumps. They even check the length of your skis, because skis which are too short will also alter the line.

Since in modern ski resorts you are almost bound to be confronted with bump fields from which there is no escape, learning how to ski them well is an essential part of your skiing development. However, as with everything we've done, effective skiing, especially as the terrain becomes more difficult, is worked on gradually, building confidence on gentle gradients. Let's look at what we already know and see how this will help us in bumps.

You know how the skis work for you and you practised tightening your turns so that you can ski in the fall line reasonably effectively. However, I don't expect you to start by skiing bumps in the fall line! Many skiers I've seen seem to think that the way to learn to ski moguls is by confronting the biggest, steepest bump field they can find, like Tortin or Mont Fort in Verbier or the 'Swiss Wall' in Champery, and struggling down. All you learn by taking that approach is to be afraid.

So the main priority is to remind ourselves about basics on an easy piste, preferably one that you know well. To begin our training for bumps, remember that nothing changes in basic technique – it is only modified. Warm up by doing a run working on rhythmic fall-line turns. Then do the same crouching as low as possible, perhaps with the hands on the knees for the first few turns. Try it again, but this time stretching as high as you can. Repeat this in a mid-stance. By this time, you should have discovered that you can change the edge of the ski in almost *any* position. Many pupils say that they find it helps to remember this when a nasty set of bumps appears ahead.

Try again the 'wobbly-knees' exercise, starting with long turns then tightening them. What you are training is the knee mobility which is essential in effective bumps skiing.

Having warmed up, what is next? Firstly, what worked for you in normal terrain will be equally effective in moguls. The skis can cope with moving over bumps at quite high speeds – they don't, as some people imagine, impale themselves! To convince yourself of this and at the same time to build awareness of how the body needs to react in bumpy terrain, try this exercise.

Choose a line of friendly bumps and just traverse across them to the other side. Notice how the body reacts – the bump *pushes* the legs up as you move over it and then as you ski into the troughs, we stretch the legs again. The first time you try it, you may find that you are being bounced around a bit. This is only because you're not used to the effects of moving at speed over moguls. What you're learning to do is to 'flatten' the bumps, by absorbing them.

Think of it this way – you anticipate the compressing effect of the bump by allowing your legs to fold and you push back into the hollow at the other side. Imagine that there is a big hand which stops your head from bouncing up as you go over the bump. You press back against it as you extend into the hollow. With practice, you will find that you can go quite fast in your traverse over the bumps, absorbing and stretching.

Experiment with slightly steeper traverses through the bumps. Try to become familiar with the feeling of the bump pushing your legs up and you pushing back down into the hollows.

The absorption or compression could be misinterpreted as 'sitting back' – but all you need to remember is to try to remain over your feet – in dynamic balance.

When we develop awareness of how the body and skis will react perfectly naturally to undulating terrain, through a traverse, we can more readily adapt what we've learned when we want to turn in bumps. As with everything else in our skiing, if we understand basic concepts from the beginning, nothing dramatically changes as we progress. Trying to trust what the ski will do for you one turn at a time and slowly is far more beneficial than attempting to string several turns together quickly at this stage. A frequent problem amongst intermediate skiers is that they try to turn too quickly in bumps. It's an understandable response to feeling intimidated by them, but is one of the worst things you can actually do.

The problem is compounded because we are often told to turn by pivoting on the crest of the bump, where ski contact with the snow is minimal. The theory is that this makes it easier to turn the ski – you pivot on top and off you go down the other side. I believe that turning on the very top of the bump complicates what happens afterwards and makes the successful completion of the turn more difficult. I say this for two reasons. For the same reason that the turn is said to be easier to start on the crest of a bump – that there is little snow contact – so it is also more difficult to stabilize the effects of the forces on us in these conditions. What typically happens is that when we set off from our pinnacle, we slither off and end up over-rotating the hips and shoulders, sometimes almost to face back uphill again, and generally feel pretty unstable. Secondly, should we try to hurry our skis through the fall line or to turn on the top of the bump, it leaves us on the steepest and most scraped part of the bump – the downhill side. If the bump is large enough, this 'front' side can be almost vertical and very icy. So we land with a fairly solid thump in the troughs, again feeling rather insecure. 'Pivoting' may seem to make sense if we are standing static – what happens when we are on the move is very different.

If we don't turn on the crest, though, where do we turn? Look at a bump field. The downhill side of the bump (I call this the front of the bump) is usually scraped, but this snow has been deposited on the uphill side (the *back*) of the bump ahead. This part is also banked in our favour. These factors will make life easier.

Again we make use of one of our very first exercises: hands on the knees, a narrow wedge, a field of *gentle* bumps. Approach the back of the first bump, pressing the knee in the direction in which you want to go. *Allow* the ski to carry you around through the fall line – the slope of the bump ahead is banked already in your favour, so use it. You aim for the soft snow deposited there so that you're moving around the side and the trough of the bump, not over the top.

Remember our 'arc' – let the skis run through the fall line and tighten the end of the turn. The arc looks like a 'fish-hook'.

Traverse or side-slip to find another line and try again. Finding a line through bumps appropriate to your skill level is an art in itself and it is one which can only be developed through practice, and perhaps by finding out the hard way! Perception can be developed, though. Going up the lift, for instance, look out for mogul slopes. Ask yourself: 'Where is the best line through that, for my standard?' Watch other skiers, seeing who takes a 'good' line. At the top of a bump run, remember to aim for the soft snow on the backs of the moguls. I see lots of intermediate skiers struggling down, turning right on the crests of bumps, or even on the icy downhill sides, simply because they haven't looked ahead (or perhaps because they've been told that this is where you do turn!). Most of all, when you are learning to ski bumps, don't expect miracles – give yourself time.

FALL-LINE SKIING IN THE BUMPS

There are many different lines you can take through a bump field. In the beginning, we practise long turns with perhaps quite long traverses in between. This is a perfectly good way of getting down and if you can do this effectively and are happy with it, there is no reason that this shouldn't be an aim in itself. Not everyone wants to be a 'freestyler' – someone who competes in very fast aggressive bump skiing straight down the fall line, with a few aerial acrobatics thrown in for good measure. However, there is no need to ski at those speeds and there is certainly no need for aggression if you want to be able to perform effective fall-line bumps skiing, providing you are fit and reasonably mobile: although there is little doubt that the older, the unfit or the very timid skier should be content with slower, longer turns through bumps (see pages 90–1 and 92–4).

It may be clearer now why I stressed the importance of making good fall-line turns on normal slopes – you need the degree of commitment which practising these turns gives, if you are to eventually learn to ski bumps well. However, as always, we shouldn't expect to do it immediately. Fall-line skiing in the bumps is very committing, so we build up confidence and awareness gradually. The skis and our bodies *will* cope, but you have to convince yourself of that. The objective here is to develop this awareness by firstly not turning at all, but by straight running. Not from the top, of course! Again find some friendly bumps, on a slope which has a good run-out (this is *very* important, as you will see) and ski down using the long turns you've been practising and stop per-haps three or four bumps from the bottom. Facing down the fall line, set off running straight, until you reach the bottom. Try it again until you feel confident about it, experiment with a different set of bumps, find a higher starting point, though don't become over-enthusiastic and go too high.

By this time, you're ready to try a few fall-line turns, again finding a starting point close to the bottom of the slope. Think *before* you set off about the line you want to take. It's too late to do it on the move. Try only two or three to begin with, turning off the banked, soft snow on the bump ahead, allowing the ski to carry you round the side and into the trough. You can control your speed by making the ends of turns tighter, and allowing the contour of the bump to slow you down.

An image which I've found helps many people in fall-line skiing through bumps, is to imagine that as we change edge to start the turn, the hips are aimed forwards and sideways towards the crest of the bump. This effectively projects the knees and hips towards the fall line.

1

2

3

4

5

6

If you recall what I said earlier, it may also help to remember that the 'block of rubber' effect in fall-line skiing helps us change edge almost automatically. The contour of the bump also helps us change edge. The bump compresses the legs, the skis carry you through the fall line and into the trough and it is here that you push back against the edged ski, to extend into the hollow. Accomplished bumps skiers can change edge whilst they're compressed, to ensure a sharp and precise start to the next turn (see picture sequence on pages 97–100). Perhaps you remember the exercises I asked you to do, crouching as low as possible, and making fall-line turns in that position? Now you can see why it is a useful form of practice for bumps skiing.

Often people get the impression that good bumps skiers 'sit back' during the compression phase. Again this is a misinterpretation.

Over bumps, the impetus tends to throw us

Look at the picture here and try it for yourself to see what I mean. If you stand up straight and then gradually bend as in the picture, you can only get down so far, before you find that you have to almost sit to stay in balance.

forward and our natural reaction is to maintain dynamic balance, creating the appearance of 'sitting back'. It is the result of *reactions* to moving over bumps, not a 'sitting back' *action*.

If by this time you feel reasonably confident about your progress, try starting your fall-line turns from higher up the slope, working on committed and positive movements.

At this stage, you may have found that you are using your poles without even thinking about it. If so, that's good! However, many people when they try fall-line bumps skiing initially, find that they get into a tangle with their poles. As before, I feel strongly that you shouldn't worry about

precisely *where* to plant the poles. Most often, this tends to happen naturally as a result of getting everything else right and specific instructions aren't helpful in any event, because there are several factors to be taken into account, such as arm length, pole length and terrain. Just remember not to block your direction of travel with the poles. As in any committed fall-line skiing, effective pole work can be of enormous help in bumps. Done well, it helps to stabilize the upper body so that we can keep facing down the fall line and use the torsional build-up of energy to its full advantage. At the same time, it gives us something to lean on as we change edge.

101

Effective use of the poles in bumps means that you have to remember that you're moving forward as you plant the pole, so really work on *stiffening* the arm as the pole hits the snow, thus 'riding over' it (see picture sequence on these pages). Feeble pole plants won't help in bumps! Good rhythm and timing are crucial, but again this is only something that you can develop through practice. It cannot be taught.

1

2

3

Problems

There will, of course, be problems. You have to expect to fall, maybe quite often, when you're learning about bumps skiing, which is one of the reasons I emphasize training on gentler slopes – falling over doesn't matter so much!

One of the most frequent problems in skiing bumps is 'over-rotation'. This means that the upper body has swung round, the hips rotate outwards, instead of leaning to the centre of the turn, the ski loses its edge and usually over you go, backwards. When you find someone lying upside down, with the heels of the skis crossed and stuck in the snow or sliding face up, head downhill, then they may – or probably may not – be comforted to know that over-rotation was the likely cause. Though what is responsible for that can in itself be due to several factors.

One cause of over-rotation is trying to turn too quickly. In our enthusiasm to get through the dreaded fall line as soon as possible, we force the skis around using physical rotation. The inside ski catches for the same reason – we push the turning ski towards the fall line and the inside edge of the other one 'hooks' us around, rotating the body even more.

Another reason could be our failure to anticipate what I call the 'stopping effect' of the bump. As we reach the back of the next bump, especially at speed, this stopping effect tends to create strong rotation, unless we stabilize the upper body by using the arms and a good solid pole plant. I sometimes ask my pupils to feel that they are really exaggerating stretching out their arms in front of them as stabilizers – and then by doing

this, they are actually adopting a normal position for fall-line skiing. Remember just because something feels exaggerated or strange, doesn't mean that it isn't right. Ineffective use of the poles can be another cause of over-rotation. If you forget to *stiffen* the arm at the moment of impact, the jolt will bend the arm backwards, turning the shoulders and the hips around with it.

Another frequent problem in bumps skiing is gathering too much speed. Two factors are responsible for control. One is the stopping effect already mentioned, which providing you anticipate it, will help you control your speed, because that part of the bump is banked already in your favour. (Hence the importance of choosing the right line.) The second means of control is by tightening the radius of the turn. This means thinking of 'fish-hooks' – tightening the end of the turn.

Don't forget that no two bump slopes are the same and the same slope can change dramatically within a day, so you should vary your line through the bumps to suit your ability, fitness and mental state. And you shouldn't become too obsessed with perfecting your fall-line bumps turns to the exclusion of everything else. I hardly ever ski the fall line in bumps when I am out for a day's free skiing, preferring to make long, fast turns instead.

One of my favourite ways of training for bumps skiing is to make long radius turns regardless of where the bumps are. This is only feasible on slopes which are not steep, because the point is to build confidence, not to undermine it. Confidence will come from the knowledge that what works for you in normal terrain will also work on more difficult slopes.

Remember also that it will take time and lots of training before a field of large bumps will lose its ogrish quality and seem quite friendly instead. Some bumps never do, even to me, so don't feel inadequate if you sometimes feel afraid. I have never lost what I think is a healthy respect for some very steep bump slopes. You will notice how much importance I place on training on terrain that doesn't have 'grizzly bears' lurking round every mogul. You cannot learn on slopes which frighten you, so don't be persuaded to attempt something which is really beyond you. I think that it is a good idea to pause sometimes, especially if it's one of those days when you're feeling tense and nothing seems to be working, and take stock of how much progress you have already made.

Once you have become a reasonably effective bumps skier, you find that the possibilities of where you can ski are that much more open.

10 ICE

Ice is top of the list of the most disliked conditions that recreational skiers have to face. Yet a fact of skiing life is that ice is something which is sooner or later unavoidable. It is partly caused by that sunshine, which we all love, melting the snow, which freezes at night and turns to ice by morning. Also we, the skiers, contribute by packing the snow down hard, and scraping the snow cover with the frequent passage of edges until the piste is honed and gleaming. So if ice is to a large extent inevitable, we should know how best to cope with it: even, dare I suggest, learn to enjoy it.

To me, ice is an extreme example of some of the difficulties that you may ordinarily face as soon as you ski on hard-packed snow. You skid excessively, feel very insecure and unbalanced. On ice, these effects are intensified. The problem is compounded by the body reacting defensively — tensing the muscles, stiffening the joints and generally making life difficult. Cramp in the feet is often a sure sign of tenseness — toes gripping the soles of the boots frantically trying to hang on. The very sound-effects of skiing on ice are intimidating: scraping, rasping noises which alert you to be on guard.

To understand these problems, we must look again at the effects of friction. We take this so much for granted in everyday life that we don't even think about how we walk or run, we just do it. Indeed, in many activities in which our bodies receive feedback through friction we can reach a reasonable level of competence with little or no formal coaching. Remember how it feels when you are walking along the street in winter and you suddenly step on a patch of ice? As we said at the very beginning, the influence of friction is considerably reduced, you slide, the body gets less feedback, becomes confused and you fall over.

When you ski you are always on a sliding base, but you can learn how to cope even though the slippery surface has reduced the positive feedback you get. If you start the turn by physical input which makes the skis skid even more on ice, the body gets very confused feedback indeed.

In softer snow, the effects of this are less noticeable because there is more resistance to the ski skidding sideways. The skis will, in these conditions, easily work for us (even if we haven't been taught how to use them to our advantage) and so the body receives enough information to be able to respond with reasonable effectiveness.

On ice, there is little resistance to the skis skidding, especially if we force them around. So what *should* we do? You often hear that you should be 'more aggressive', 'attack' or 'fight' the mountain. To me, nothing could be less appropriate to skiing in general, and is particularly inappropriate to skiing on ice.

Firstly, think of skiing in curves, and not sharp skidded angles. You should think of edges. *Allow* the skis to run on their edges; use them as they were designed to be used, to turn you, and you will find that the degree of sideways skid, which causes your problems on ice, is reduced.

Secondly, commit yourself at the beginning of the turn, but do so *gently*. Soft but progressive movements are needed. Soft, because any physically strong movement will only produce skidding in these conditions. Progressive, because it helps control. The more softly and precisely we can change edge at the beginning of the turn, the greater the chance of control at the end. Physical force, on ice, will only make you feel less secure than ever. Think instead of skiing on eggs; any hard movements and they will break.

Thirdly, you also often hear that you should 'put more weight on your downhill ski' when skiing on ice. If you already have started to skid, then physically putting more weight on the skidding ski doesn't help. Remember weight distribution on skis is a result of the forces that are set up by us travelling at speed in the turn and the positions we need to adopt to react to them. If you try to put more weight on one ski, you will lose the edge that you need to keep control.

Having said all of this, I would not expect to ski very well on ice either, unless my skis were able to do the job. You don't need to buy a special pair of skis. Good models are now being designed to cope in all conditions. Whatever skis you have, it is essential that for skiing on ice, their edges should be sharp, to give the 'grip' which will help you.

11 POWDER

Tracks in soft snow.

The classic dream of most skiers is a vision of skiing through untracked deep snow in the sunshine, casting sparkling plumes of fluffy powder upwards and feeling as if you're floating on a cloud. But many recreational skiers have convinced themselves that this is a dream which never comes true. 'Skiing the powder' well is often portrayed as the mark of distinction which sets the experts apart from the rest. But I believe that having reached this point, almost any recreational skier can learn to cope well with deeper snow, by applying what we have already discovered.

Firstly, however, there are many misunderstandings and psychological inhibitions which can cause problems before we even set foot – or skis – into deep snow. Sometimes we feel apprehensive. Despite the images of soft, light-as-air snow, many people are afraid of venturing into it. It may be fear of the unknown – the 'what if' factor. Not being able to see one's skis, or what lies under the snow can also have inhibiting effects. Fear of speed and of falling compound the apprehension. Add to these the many misconceptions about technique for skiing in powder snow and it isn't surprising that so many skiers get discouraged.

Many of the misconceptions come about because you're often told that the technique for skiing deep snow is different. For instance, if you watch an effective skier coming towards you through deep snow, the visual impression can be completely misleading. You see the feet and legs apparently being pushed from side to side. Indeed, this is often taught. In normal piste conditions, it is possible to do this and achieve a reasonable simulation of good skiing, because the skis can skid sideways. In deep snow, if your concept of turning is to push the skis sideways in a physically-induced skid, it won't work because there is resistance to this movement, which is why many skiers have difficulties in these conditions. The tracks left by effective skiers in soft snow are curves or 'S' shapes – the skis follow their length, carrying the feet from side to side. This is what is responsible for our impression of the feet being 'pushed' sideways.

Another misconception about powder-snow skiing is that you should 'sit back'. It is an impression which when copied is responsible for much fatigue and painful thigh muscles. What is responsible for the 'sitting back' impression can be explained by the pictures below (see also pp 112–13).

In contrast to what happens on a hard-packed slope, in deep snow when the skis move at speed, the tips tend to come up to the surface – they begin to 'plane'. It is this effect which creates the illusion of the skier actively trying to sit back. Again, it is a *reaction*, in this case to speed in deep snow and is not primarily a physically-induced action by the skier. It may be necessary in certain circumstances, which depend on the depth and the consistency of the snow and the gradient of the slope, to very slightly adjust your weight backwards to begin with in order to overcome the resistance of the snow and to allow you to gather speed. This allows the skis to plane to the surface. But thereafter it is a question of remaining in dynamic balance. As usual, a static interpretation of what happens when we are moving will not help our skiing.

Other instructions about skiing in deep snow tell you to put your weight evenly on both feet. As with many things in skiing, this is another example of an observation of a *reaction*, which is then taken apart and taught as an *action*.

In deep snow, there is no firm base and as we turn, the resultant force creates fairly even pressure over both skis. It is not necessary to think about actively doing this – it will happen as a result of the forces in the turn. I would like to add here that I believe these considerations only really matter in very deep snow, the 'bottomless powder' of exceptional conditions.

You are also told to keep your feet together in deep snow. The reason given is that the snow will separate the skis so that they cross or otherwise get into a tangle. But if your skis are wandering off in different directions, then something is going wrong in basic technique and no amount of forcing the feet together will cure the problem.

FIRST STEPS IN DEEP SNOW

Our mental images of deep snow skiing conjure up pictures of effortlessness and grace, but you cannot copy these. What you can do, though, is to copy what creates what you see. As you progress, it is also worth remembering that your mental commitment will be tested as you move into unfamiliar territory. This is why it is important not to over-complicate things, especially when you first venture into deep snow. Powder skiing, in particular, suffers from an unnecessary mystique about 'special' technique. As in everything else I've explained, what we learn at the beginning does not change as we become more advanced. Sound basic technique only needs slight modification to allow us to adapt to new challenges of terrain and snow conditions.

There are many ways to enjoy skiing in deep snow. As with bumps skiing, you don't have to ski down the steepest slopes in the fall line, nor do you even have to be a particularly good fall-line skier. To me, to this day, one of the greatest pleasures in skiing is to just run straight or traverse through deep snow (see pages 116 and 117).

To appreciate what does happen in powder-snow skiing, we have to bear in mind that the skis will work for us in deep snow as they did in other conditions. And – this perhaps is the most committing factor – we need greater speed to get through deep snow. The energy required to help the skis work comes from speed and not from us as a physical action.

Beginning to cope with powder, however, can be approached in the same way as we have done before – experimenting gradually with what we already know will work for us, in different situations. If you are lucky enough, you may wake up one morning to a covering of powder snow on the marked runs and then is the best time to get out early and play with some of our earlier exercises. You should *never* leave the marked skiing area alone, or with inexperienced people.

Simply straight running or traversing are excellent ways to develop a feeling for deeper snow. Take a dive into it. Deliberately falling around in soft snow may seem like a second childhood, but it helps us to lose some of our fears about skiing in powder. Try running from the piste into the soft snow off to the sides and back again, feeling the slowing down and the acceleration.

Learning to turn in deep snow involves no mystery. The first sensations may seem different, but you shouldn't mistake this as a signal that you need to ski differently. To show that the ski will still work for you as usual, we return to the wee wedge and work through the first exercises, especially hands-on-the-knees and reaching-out.

At this stage, as you may have already noticed, you should also be prepared to fall, perhaps quite a lot. If you think of falling in deep snow as a nuisance, then you will have problems! Pupils have often said that despite the first attempts, when every turn one way seemed to be accompanied by a fall in the other direction, the frustration was more than made up for by the turns when everything was right and they felt that they understood what I meant when I said that 'nothing changes'.

When I take people into deep snow for their first few runs, I ask them to use long radius turns. They are less committing and give you more time to think. I think that it's also essential not even to consider keeping the skis parallel – on the contrary, I encourage the 'wee plough'. Pressing in

the knee to help you turn may seem awfully elementary, but it helps to short circuit the built-in habits which the brain has stored away and which creep on us when we're least aware. Resist the urge to turn the skis by physical force. Be prepared to accept the fact that they will accelerate towards the fall line and remember that control comes at the end of the turn. If you practise at slower speeds to begin with, you will soon gain the confidence to allow the skis to run faster. This speed will help you to turn.

As you ski faster, you will notice more that at the end of every turn there is a kind of 'stopping' effect as the force makes the skis sink into the snow. Because the skis cannot go sideways through deep snow, the 'stopping' effect on us is greater and we need to resist it more, to stop it from pulling us over. The 'reaching out' exercise can help us to counteract this.

FALL-LINE SKIING IN POWDER

If you can ski effective fall-line turns on hard-packed snow, you should be able to adapt what you have learned to powder snow quite easily. There are a few things to be prepared for, however, which may unsettle you until you become more familiar with the sensations of skiing the fall line in powder snow. Again speed is an essential, but committing, ingredient. And be aware that the force pulling you to the outside of the turn in deeper snow feels quite exaggerated until you become used to it.

At this stage, if you can recall when you first practised fall-line skiing, the forces that are generated actually *help* us to perform effectively. Visualize good performers and remember that they make it look effortless because they use the

existing forces to their advantage. The 'block of rubber' effect, I think, is an important image to keep in mind.

The faster we travel, the greater are the forces in the turn. In deep snow, this means that the pressure exerted by these forces on the skis makes the skis sink further into the snow. The body crosses the line of travel of the skis at the end of the turn and the release of pressure changes edges for us.

Just as we needed to anticipate the effects of bumps skiing, so we should be ready for similar

sensations but this time in different terrain. Sound pole work does help, but I can only remind you that it shouldn't become a fixation to the detriment of your skiing. I know many good powder-snow skiers who don't rely upon a strong pole plant in these conditions.

The feeling of the skis 'shooting forward' is again, as it was in bumps skiing, a *reaction* to what is happening. If you watch an accomplished powder-snow skier swooping downhill, it is easy to misinterpret this pure reaction as a direct physical action by the skier.

The feeling is that the skis shoot forwards towards the fall line and to the surface of the snow, with a considerable degree of impetus if we are travelling fast. This produces what is sometimes referred to as a 'bouncing' feeling.

119

Another adaptation of deep-snow technique is often referred to as 'down' unweighting. In bumps skiing we absorb the force created by hitting a bump and allow the legs to compress during the edge change and then extend the legs during the turn. So, as the snow gets deeper, and we ski steeper slopes or simply go faster, the force at the end of the turn pulls us further into the snow. This creates a 'sinking' effect. *As* we initiate our next turn and move towards the fall line, the skis will rise to the surface.

The force of the skis coming to the surface should be absorbed by letting the legs compress and then extending them against the edges to complete the turn.

Look at the profile of our tracks through the snow (left). It's almost like looking at a series of bumps. In fact, as we ski faster in deep snow, this is exactly how it should be treated. The end result is an impression of effortlessness, but is caused by you, the skier, harnessing the working of the ski and the energy which comes from speed to your advantage.

WHAT CAN GO WRONG

At this moment, you may feel, as a struggling newcomer to powder show, that the last thing you want to be told is that it is helpful to allow yourself greater speed. I don't think I am being unrealistic if I tell you that I believe that with the right training and commitment, the speed to ski powder is *well* within the capabilities of the keen holiday skier. It may be difficult to believe entirely at this stage until you feel it happening, but moving faster will actually *help* overcome some of the problems you experience. Like anything else, however, you have to build up gradually and not expect too much until you become accustomed to the feel of powder-snow skiing.

There are other more specific problems which you may find are inhibiting your progress. They may have several and interlocking causes, but some of the more common problems encountered are easily identified. A frequent source of trouble, for instance, is, again, over-rotation. This is often manifested in skis crossing. The source of this is often trying to physically turn the skis into the fall line; the turning ski is pushed ahead of the other ski and then they both cross, with the usual result. This is sometimes complicated by the feeling of not being able to see your skis. Even if we succeed in getting through the fall line, a second effect lies lurking – the inside ski hooks and sends us spiralling backwards to the outside of the turn. This is one of the commonest of all deep snow falls. I emphasize commitment as part of the solution, because it helps us to remember to trust that the ski will turn us if it is edged and we are ready to respond – providing that you don't try to rush the turn.

The habit of shifting weight is another problem in deep-snow skiing. As we have observed so often before, if you try physically to transfer pressure on to the turning ski, it will flatten and sink into the snow. This will either rotate us around out of our bindings, or take us off down the slope at some speed, since flat skis don't turn. Do you remember what I said earlier about concepts of turning? My bindings are set at the lowest setting possible in *all* conditions and speeds – if *my* concept of turning was to rotate the ski around, I would twist out of the bindings at every turn!

It is worth reminding ourselves that many difficulties in skiing, not just in deep snow, are due to our lack of awareness of the effects of the forces set up in the turn. To go back to basics for a moment, any heavy object travelling at speed in a curve is subjected to a force to the outside of that curve. On hard-packed snow, that will mean for most of us a greater degree of sideways movement. But in deep snow, that sideways motion – the skid – is largely prevented and so the effect of the force, at the end of the turn especially, is more noticeable. To understand this properly, you only have to look at where most falls in powder snow happen – to the outside of the turn, leaving us rather inelegantly pinned on our backs. What causes this rotation is the effect of the force pulling our hips (the centre of mass of the body) outwards.

There are other inhibitions which we can suffer in powder snow, some of which we have already touched upon, like not being able to see your skis. Training ourselves to trust what the skis are doing under the snow, if we allow them to work for us, is the surest cure I know for this problem. Another less obvious feature of deep-snow skiing is that it will not always take place in brilliant sunshine and perfect visibility. Occasionally, that untracked paradise can be encountered under quite different conditions of heavy snowfalls, cloud cover and high winds. Again I can only say that effective technique learned from a basic level is the most secure defence. Awareness that the ski will work for you regardless of bad light and difficult terrain has helped many people. You may think it is perverse, but I consider that skiing in poor conditions actually helps me to maintain my standard of skiing.

Equipment . . .

Of course, equipment helps the skier too. Double lens goggles are essential, together with a pocket full of tissues and supplemented by a tube of good anti-mist. Many people have an utterly miserable time because they have inadequate eye protection in these conditions. Clothing too matters in deep-snow skiing. One-piece, Gore-tex suits keep out the snow and wetness and long-cuffed gloves stop the snow from getting inside and freezing your hands. Obvious precautions, perhaps, but ones which are surprisingly often overlooked.

The type of ski you choose can also affect your performance in deep snow, if you are less than expert. Softer skis, because they bend more readily, will make life easier for you in deep snow. But they should still be of a reasonable length.

. . . and losing it

There is another aspect of deep-snow skiing that deserves a special mention. If you go to a ski resort in springtime, after the snow has melted, you would probably be amazed at the number of ski poles and lone skis found in areas where people have skied in deep snow during winter, not to mention other diverse bits and pieces. Falling in deep snow can be a very frustrating experience if in doing so you lose your skis, poles and other equipment and don't know the correct way of looking for them. There *is*, yes, a correct method! Skis are obviously the most important things to locate, since it is a serious matter if you have to

walk out of a powder field. I follow a set routine religiously when I fall and lose skis. (I *do* fall, usually in quite a spectacular way, and hence my skis can end up surprisingly far away.)

First check that you are in one piece and don't try to leap up immediately. Find out what is missing. It's unusual to lose both skis and poles, so there is often one of them at hand to help you in the next stage. Feel around you carefully in case the missing equipment is nearby. I emphasize CAREFULLY here, since if you jump up and start thrashing around, the chances are that you will end up burying whatever is lost for good, or at least until springtime. Failing that, look at your tracks before you go any further and *try to remember* where you fell. You can often tell from the snow. If you have friends around, organize them into a line abreast and, starting at least 10–20 metres below where you fell, get them to 'slice' the snow in a criss-cross section with the heel of a ski.

Skis once released can travel in a straight line

quite a long way under the snow and can also come to rest on their sides, so it is important to be thorough and give yourself a good margin of error. Alternatives which have been suggested include fitting security straps long enough to prevent any dangerous whiplash, or long, luminous nylon cords attached to your ski, with the other end unattached, but retained in your trouser leg! This could save a lot of time and inconvenience, not to say potential danger from getting stuck on a mountain side without your skis. Getting up after a fall is also not quite as simple as it is on hard snow. The snow tends to fall away from you with every movement and you sink further into it. Try to pack the snow down around you to make a more stable platform from which you can put on your skis. Don't be in a hurry. If you flounder around trying to reattach your equipment too quickly, you will only as likely as not fall over again. As you might have noticed, getting up in powder snow is quite tiring. Once you are up, do remember to clear all the packed snow away from the sole of your boot before putting on your ski again.

SAFETY OFF THE BEATEN TRACK

To ski in the winter wilderness of the mountains is the dream of many skiers. It is perhaps their ultimate goal. And as resorts become busier every year, more and more skiers turn towards the great open spaces which lie in the distance. 'Off-piste' can mean skiing within a few yards of the runs or venturing further afield. (Ski touring is in its own category, involving extensive mileage and days and nights spent high up in the mountains.) However near or far you go off-piste, the attraction which these mountain areas has for skiers seems to be magnetic and there are nowadays more than just a few people who risk their own and other's lives by going there unprepared.

It is not unusual for skiers to take off into unmarked areas in complete ignorance of mountain dangers and with little awareness of what might befall them. My advice is to only go off-piste with those who are qualified to take you there – *mountain* guides who spend years studying and training before they achieve their qualification, or professional, fully-qualified ski teachers, who also have additional training and mountain experience.

This does not mean party leaders, perhaps supplied by tour operators or ski clubs, or teachers with lesser qualifications. A properly organized group will also have the necessary equipment which it is essential to take. It should go without saying that it is suicidal to go off-piste alone, as the records of the piste patrols annually show. Beware also friends claiming a little experience. Many are the groups who have been caught in avalanches because their friends went down the same slope the day before or that morning or even last year and said that it was 'safe'. *Do* familiarize yourself with the warnings put up by the ski patrols when avalanche risk is present – *and heed them.* The patrols will close some marked runs too if there is general avalanche danger, so look around you to check this.

If all of this seems dramatic, then it is said with the knowledge that if the joys of skiing off the beaten track are easy to see, then its dangers are equally real, if less obvious, because they lurk in wait for the unaware. It is often argued by highly-qualified mountain guides, the more one skis off-piste the greater the probability of one day being caught in an avalanche.

ALI ROSS SKIING CLINICS

Many people are surprised when they find out that I still teach intermediate skiers myself. I think they expect that I coach only race trainees, for example, or other quite advanced skiers. This book has been devoted to showing you that anyone can learn to ski effectively. My aim in the Skiing Clinics is the same – to help you, the recreational skier, understand what *creates* good skiing.

The Skiing Clinics are held in France and Switzerland during winter and in the French resort of Tignes during summer. There are normally two clinics per week, open to intermediate and more advanced skiers. A typical week's course might look like this. After arrival in the resort on the Saturday, and a day free to find your ski legs on the Sunday, there is a detailed introduction to the Clinic's programme on Sunday evening before dinner. This gives everyone the chance to meet the other members of the Clinic and to ask me any questions that you may have.

Tuition begins on the Monday and finishes on the following Friday. I class pupils as far as possible with others of comparable ability. One group is taught in the morning and one in the afternoon, and each receives at least two and a half hours concentrated tuition from me on the slopes every day. Built into the programme, therefore, is also time to practise what you have learned, either with the other members of your group or by yourself, as you prefer, in time for the next day's clinic. These practice times are a very important part of learning progress, if you are to get the most out of the week's programme.

Part of the week's skiing will be videotaped and this will be used to help you understand how you can improve your skills.

After the day's skiing, you will be able to consolidate what you have learned and to ask any questions which you may have, in the early evening seminar, which I hold most weekday evenings. On 'video' days, the tape is replayed and analysed during the evening seminar so that you will have the chance to see yourself in action. The seminars usually last for a minimum of one hour.

For the Intermediate Clinic you should already be able to ski a red run, using linked turns, though not necessarily parallel.

The intermediate clinic will deal with:

- review of basic skils;
- problem analysis;
- moving off the learning 'plateau'.

For the Advanced Clinic you should already be capable of skiing a red run confidently using basic parallel turns.

The advanced clinic will cover:

- review of basic skills;
- problem analysis;
- development and refinement of technique for difficult terrain and snow conditions;
- powder skiing, if conditions permit.

There are also Intensive Clinics designed to develop and refine your technique for difficult terrain. There will be one group of ten per week for advanced skiers only. The services of local top mountain guides will be used when necessary. I advise a reasonable degree of physical fitness for all courses, but is especially important if you are considering one of the advanced skiers' weeks.

FINAL THOUGHTS

I never thought of this as a 'how to do it' book. But I do feel that once we have understood what creates good skiing, we have the foundations which will help us learn to be 'unlimited skiers'. The other things of importance we can never learn from a book – feedback, encouragement and our own awareness of how we learn.

I hope that as the first frosts of autumn spark off memories, excitement and anticipation of skiing, the words here may contribute to the goal of most skiers, which is to spend many, more years enjoying this sport, whatever the conditions.